S0-BJR-327

An Ordinary Marriage

HARRIET ROBEY

An Atlantic Monthly Press Book

Little, Brown and Company   Boston/Toronto

FIRST EDITION

Library of Congress Cataloging in Publication Data
Robey, Harriet.
    An ordinary marriage.
    "An Atlantic Monthly Press book."
    1. Robey, Harriet.   2.Wives—United States—
Biography.   3.Marriage—United States—Case studies.
I. Title.
HQ759.R625—1984   306.8'1'0924   84–12580
ISBN 0–316–75127–8

ATLANTIC-LITTLE, BROWN BOOKS
ARE PUBLISHED BY
LITTLE, BROWN AND COMPANY
IN ASSOCIATION WITH
THE ATLANTIC MONTHLY PRESS

BP

Designed by Patricia Girvin Dunbar

Published simultaneously in Canada by
Little, Brown & Company (Canada) Limited

PRINTED IN THE UNITED STATES OF AMERICA

An Ordinary Marriage

Also by Harriet Robey

Bay View — A Summer Portrait
There's a Dance in the Old Dame Yet

To my four children, who aided, abetted, and approved as I flung open the doors of my past to gain freedom from myself and become a happy maverick.

Contents

Foreword

MY WRITING has developed out of a need to know. My first book was privately published in 1980. It was a study of ancestral character traits that still persist in my extended family. I did not realize at the time I wrote it that I was searching out my own roots, my own identity. I found it.

My second book, *There's a Dance in the Old Dame Yet,* was published two years later. Here I dealt with my widowhood and old age, and my rediscovered capacity for life and growth. They came. I also found a curious mental youth again. But the last words of that book were, "Oh, Alec! Alec!" I wondered at the time why I thus cried out so impulsively to my husband's memory.

This third book began as soon as the second was in the hands of the publisher. It deals with the unfinished business of that cry — with my marriage to Alec, with my guilt and anger over his death, and, ultimately, with the meaning of love. As I wrote the book, I found myself using the enigmatic Mona Lisa as a sort of medium. Through her my marriage to Alec stood out in bold relief. From her I grasped the meaning of the imperatives within the human psyche: survival, mating, reproduction, genetic improvement, the union of the yin and yang, the need to create. to know, and the drive to achieve true integrity regardless of convention. I have seized upon these imperatives and so have found who, why, and what, as woman, I am. With this discovery has come a revival. I am in awe of the potential grace in the soul of humankind.

I express deep gratitude for the literary vision of Upton Brady, my patient editor, who has read the entire text aloud for our joint corrections; to Llewellyn Howland, my agent and periodic critic; and to my son and daughter — the Ames Robeys — with their, to me, astounding word-processing computer. All have been my eyes, my organizers, and my support, and without them this book could not have been completed.

Finally, I am painfully aware of the dangers of autobiography, not the least of which is that fiction and fantasy are as important in the life of the mind as is "objective fact." I have reported here my life as I lived it, but I would be the last to claim that this narrative is either "objective" or entirely "factual."

PART ONE

Upon my word, the happiest day of my life was the most miserable morning I ever passed in the whole course of my existence. We commenced crying at church. My father cried when he gave me away; Charles cried when he took me for his wedded wife; and I cried when I took him for my wedded husband; and the bridesmaids cried because everyone else cried.

* * *

At breakfast, Papa made us all cry when he wished us joy for the remainder of our days. Charles cried when he thanked Papa for the pleasing things he had said, and the joy that had been heaped upon us; and when the time came for Charles and myself to withdraw to the Continent, every soul, down to the very servants, cried, as if I were about to be handed over to the executioner, instead of the arms of my dear Charles.

— From *Whom to Marry and How
to Get Married*, edited by the
Brothers Mayhew

CHAPTER I

Wooing and Wedding

IT IS THAT so rare a day in June, 1923, our wedding day! I am the princess, the true princess at last, in passionate blinding love for the first time in my twenty-two years. I am in ecstasy.

Since Alec Robey is an only child, Mrs. Robey has taken me to her bosom as I have her to mine. I adore her. She is fine and wonderful and knows everything. I'm also half in love with gentle Dr. Robey. Yes, we will all live happily forever, for we are like marrying like, the best chance for a blissful marriage.

I stand alone in the empty hall of my home waiting for Father to join me. The last of the cars has crunched down the gravel drive and ours waits at the front door. The six bridesmaids (all first cousins) are like a departing bouquet of flowers. Mother and my sister — too pregnant to be my matron-of-honor — and her husband went in the family car and in the last, Dr. and Mrs. Robey and my Alec. Yes, Mrs. Robey said Alec could see me in my bridal finery. He took me into the study and handed me a red velvet oblong box with glinting-white satin lining that held a delicate string of small pink pearls, real ones perfectly matched and graduated in size. He fastened the diamond clasp at the nape of my neck by holding the lace aside and softly kissed me there.

In this part of the house there is silence. Some male voices come from the kitchen wing — a shout of laughter — the caterers from Boston. I look in the great Victorian wall mirror. My dress is exquisite, the long train banded with yards of family rose-point lace that comes to a peak in my hair, held in a circle of orange blossoms. I wear something old, something new, something borrowed, something blue. My very pointed white satin slippers come from the Fifth Avenue Andrew Alexander Shoe Store which Mrs. Robey now owns and oversees. Alec and I made the trip to New York just to get those slippers and we saw Somerset Maugham's *Rain,* starring Jeanne Eagels (my first Broadway play), and I wept and was afraid.

I timidly touch the pearls. I am a pearl of great price. I am innocent and trusting and without guile and so beautiful, and the mirror gives back a vision of bridal purity. I am ready, incandescent with a halo of joy, ready for sacrifice. The mirror image goes all wavy and misty. I look away and go to the door of the living room. It is now strangely empty of furniture, but the whole mantel in front of which we'll stand to receive is one enormous mass of color. Poor tired Mother picked and arranged the flowers early this morning — I saw her from my window down in her sunken garden, which had once been the manure pit of the great old farm barn — brilliant delft blue delphinium and peonies of a red raspberry-jelly clarity, almost luminous.

I turn and wander through the dining room into the playroom of our childhood, my veil and train over my arm. The room has a fireplace and windows on three sides. My eyes are drawn to the east, which looks out on the old fieldstone wall that the settlers made and where the black snakes live. I never would climb over that tumbly wall but I was proud if I found a particularly large crisp and crinkly shed skin near it. Am I still afraid of snakes?

I can't face all this gorgeous display which has followed upon the issuance of our wedding invitations; completing a romance which began on a small, slow Cunarder, Southampton to Boston, and which for me featured a man called Alec Robey playing the grand piano to a maid who sat and listened adoringly. His playing was chiefly Debussy's "The Girl With the Flaxen Hair" as he looked at me. Or he rippled chords, never dissonant, and told me of the girl, Ethel, in Connecticut he was coming home to propose to. And at night, the ocean calm, the air sea-fresh, the full moon brilliant, the talk was of life and of his year's adventure at Oxford (a cultural filling sandwiched between two years at Harvard Business School). And his traveling with his parents through the Continent for a few weeks. Meanwhile, I had been doing the same with my uncle, aunt, and cousin who had just graduated from Smith. I told him my history, which was quite an empty one — and how I had just graduated in June from Bryn Mawr.

He told me more about Ethel and I had to be very firm with myself, for he was the handsomest, finest, straightest, strongest man I had ever met, one who could tear a telephone book in two or break a finger when he shook hands, he told me. Muscles rippled at every motion.

We parted at the dock, each looking back at the other. Let him have his old Connecticut Ethel.

In two months came an invitation to the Harvard-Dartmouth game, my first. His mother was having a luncheon for about twenty of Alec's friends. The day was heaven and I was adorned with Alec's corsage of red roses. Soon Mrs. Robey invited me to certain cultural occasions — she obviously approved of me and certainly she admired my distinguished uncle and aunt, Harvard Professor Oakes Ames and his wife, Blanche. Connecticut Ethel was never mentioned again. Letters began between us and he visited me in the country. There was now no stopping the wildly escalating passion.

Then came the night of decision, the night of our first kiss. Then the engagement announcement, the invitations, the presents, all ending up in this room. I had run in a flash through the reverie of a wooing and winning. It was right.

Now I can look, I can focus. The old playroom glows with gold, crystal, and silver. Everyone is rich nowadays, particularly the Robey friends. Damask-covered trestle tables line the walls. In the center of our old play table (Father had it made with four drawers, one for each of us to keep our treasures in) and on the delicate damask was my sterling, twelve of everything. Mrs. Robey helped me pick the design. But with Alec earning $50 a week, would we ever serve oysters on the half shell to a twelve-guest dinner? Such cute little forks! But Mrs. Robey is to give us $2,000 a year and my parents the same, and we will have Uncle Tom's house free.

Glinting, sparkling, and mine — all mine — no, ours. But all addressed to me. I am a princess out of the fairy stories.

All the good fairies have sent rich presents. So far, five Tiffany silver bowls, big ones, seven steak sets, one Tiffany and one Bigelow and Kennard sterling bureau set (including rouge or cream pots, nail buffers, and even shoe-button hooks), everything initialed. But there is a cake basket so ill shaped, so ornately embossed and chased, that the eyes stay on it in disbelief. Surely this comes from the angry evil fairy. When we take it back to the store to have the initials removed that we might give it to someone we're obligated to but whom we dislike, they say, "No, the silver is thin as tissue paper there. The initials have been removed too many times."

On a corner table are the rather trivial presents from our contemporaries: a vase, a trivet, a cake cutter, bookends. I am suddenly ashamed of my scorn. Scattered around there are discreet gold-edged cards saying, "Gift $100" or "Gift $500." They lie among the dozens of dinner plates, after-dinner coffee cups, crystal, glassware, books, trays, lamps, and a few antiques.

Alas, there is no present from Uncle Tom, my second father, the giver of all good things (including a canoe, a horse, a little

6

Colt revolver, a small sailboat). He's been ill and is taking early retirement to return to Rhode Island, where he was born. I don't know what his illness is and I don't think of him much anymore.

From the hall, Father calls, "Time!"

"Coming!"

I find myself moving as if I might break. Father and our Mary O'Connor help me into my grandparents' limousine, adjust my train on my lap, and I open the white box, my bouquet — a mass of lilies of the valley just such as Father gave Mother when they were married and has given her on every anniversary since. In the two and one-half months of decision-making since our engagement, I have insisted on only that one thing.

During the fifteen-minute drive to Saint Anne's Episcopal Church in Lowell, I am in a daze. Yet associations flow. We don't speak, Father and I, for we don't know what to say and he never talks to make conversation and never speaks of feelings. He, like Mother, is not much interested in small talk. I can feel my love pouring out toward the Robeys, the doctor so very tall but flat-chested, unlike Alec, very quiet like Father and someone to stay close to; she such a magnificent, handsome woman with early snow-white hair and brilliant clothes and her authoritative knowledge of everything social and intellectual and artistic. In fact, Mrs. Robey is almost too generous and too kind to me, and I follow her slavishly. Already she has indoctrinated me in certain social amenities and formalities. She has saved Mother so many trips to the city, for Mother is suffering badly from her neuralgia. She has handed me over to Mrs. Robey in a way, just as she handed me over to Uncle Tom once.

Mrs. Robey knows that Saturday high noon is the most stylish time for a formal wedding. She has ordered the wedding invitations with classic script. My wedding dress is designed and made by her couturier, my hair permanented — perhaps a bit

7

too tightly — by her hair stylist, the caterer is the best in Boston, and the florist for the bouquets is her favorite. Bachrach, of course, is the photographer. And her adored divine of the Old South Church, George Angier Gordon, will naturally pronounce us man and wife. No one else could do for her beloved son.

A marriage made in heaven, the only difference being my lack of sophistication. There had been one potential moment of dispute, but here Mother had her way in her own house. The putteed chauffeurs bringing Robey friends from the city need not have the full-course dinner. Sandwiches, coffee, and ice cream would do for them on tables set up in the arborvitae-enclosed laundry yard with the lines taken down. Mother doesn't care for chauffeurs, limousines, or formal social weddings. She's a simple lady and a lovely one.

"She's shy like me," I tell Mrs. Robey, who is genuinely puzzled that Mother will have nothing to do with Colonial Dames, the D.A.R., or even the Social Register. Of course I would get into the Social Register as her son's wife.

Alec's love for his mother and her adoration of him are so beautiful that I will never shatter their relationship — if I can help it. And yet his love is mine, too. Our love letters have the sweetness of the Song of Solomon. And this morning I locked them all in Uncle Tom's mahogany cigar humidor, which he gave me when he stopped smoking. I see again Alec's strong calligraphy in his letter — written on Easter Day when our engagement was formally announced at a big reception at the Robeys'. With it came a piece of mosaic.

Darling,

Flowers pass and fade away, yet this rose lives through all the years. Its petals are tinged with a delicate hue, with a love that cannot fade. Oh, Hap dear, this is no cold dull slab, a pleasing creation of art, but a sign, a symbol, a sacred glory in my heart.

8

I have heard the mavis singing its love song to the morn, I've seen the dew-drops clinging to the rose just newly born . . .

Doubtless you have a mosaic piece like this from Florence where the Arno rolls. Yet I thought, Dearest, you might be pleased with this, the loveliest work I could find in all the city. There are no greens, blues, or colors such as you particularly like, in this, but do you care for it enough to accept it, Beloved, with my love impressed upon it?

'Gainst death, and all-oblivious enmity shall you pace forth: your praise shall still find room, even in the eyes of all posterity that wear this world out to the unending doom. So, till the judgment that yourself arise, you live in this and swell in lover's eyes. It is my love that keeps mine eye awake, mine own true love that doth my rest defeat to play the watchman ever for thy sake. For the watch I keep whilst thou dost wake elsewhere, from me far off, with others all too near. This stone speaks sweeter than my tongue — the world of love for thee.

From your own,
Shap

And then my letter, in small and delicate and rather faint handwriting.

That thou mayst not forget me in the long week that followeth, and that thou mayst remember that I do love thee truly, so do I now write to thee in these few words, to remind thee of a heart and mind and body which turn to thee in everything, for they exist not without thee.

How could I have been afraid of love before?

At the church there is a little crowd of onlookers outside the marquee. The organ is softly burbling out its chords. Mrs. Robey is just going down the aisle on my brother's arm. Her dress is solid blue lace to the floor, her hat enormous with proud ostrich plumes. She is magnificent. Dr. Robey and Howard Leaman, the family's closest friend and financial adviser, settle in the right front pew. Silently I call out to my mother-in-law as did the Biblical Ruth, "Intreat me not to leave thee or to return from following after thee, for whither thou goest I will go; and where thou lodgest, I will lodge; thy people shall be my people and thy God my God." Next Mother is taken down. Her long dress is simple mouse-gray and beautifully cut. There is a dashing little tilt to the brim of her soft green velvet hat. That's like Mother. If you have to be conspicuous, do it well.

There is silence. Then the wedding march begins. The ushers flow down two by two. And then the bridesmaids follow to that most awkward of music, step — hesitate, step — hesitate. And now standing up there are Alec, his best man, two ministers, the bridesmaids and ushers. Two of these detach themselves and unroll the long white train protector even to my feet.

All faces, a pale pink blur, are now turned back toward the entrance. This is the moment. I take Father's arm, gentle little Father's arm, and I proudly, in all my bride-pride beauty and glow, walk the gauntlet of appraising eyes. Is it Father's arm or mine that trembles? His club foot beats a slight, soft thud-thump as we walk slowly and solemnly, looking straight ahead. Oh Father, Father, remember those days when I ran down the little slope to the garage when I heard your car come home at night and we walked back in step, my hand reaching up to hold yours and jointly we chanted, "Hayfoot, strawfoot, belly full of bean soup" and laughed together? Though when you tried to help me with assignments in Greek and Latin in adolescence I froze and became an idiot. Yet I wanted so to learn with you instead of Uncle Tom.

And there ahead is Alec, waiting. I come to rest beside him. Father fades away with the music, a hush — and a sonorous voice, "Dearly Beloved, we are gathered . . ." The exquisite, ecstatic moment of destiny, about to become one flesh, and I am joyful to submit to this beautiful man as unto the Lord.

I hear Alec's voice and mine repeating dutifully, "I will" and

"I do." But at some point — will I ever know when or where? — as Dr. Gordon is speaking, I look at "my minister," he whom I met only yesterday at the rehearsal, and with my left eye I wink at him in an uncontrollable wink. I hold the wink for one, two, three seconds while my right eye stares meaningfully into his startled face. A God-awful wink without rhyme or reason! What had I done! How could I? All bride-beauty gone now. Desperate in my self-consciousness I finish up as a witless automaton.

The final benediction — "The Lord lift up His countenance upon you and give you peace, both now and in the life everlasting. Amen." The organ peals out, my bouquet is placed in my hand, my train is turned with me. Alec and I walk fast, faster, my arm in his, down that long aisle and out into dazzling noon sunlight, I having promised a loving, cleaving, obedient subjection until death. We are forever one. Let joy be unconfined and let me forget that wink forever.

CHAPTER 2

Honeymoon — The First Awareness

ℐT'S LATE afternoon when we reach my family's summer cottage, Bay View, on the lip of the ocean at Cape Ann.

Such fun — we outwitted the bridal party and their deep-laid plans for mischief. Puss Leaman sat in his limousine talking to Father, who stood on the stoop. We dashed out and piled in as Mr. Leaman got out the far door. The chauffeur drove off with a scattering of gravel and we picked up the Ford Runabout hidden in the woods. Here we have four days before our boat sails for Italy and my uncle's villa on Lake Como.

Lucy, our maid since my baby days, welcomes us. She is to cook and make the bed, since I can't cook at all. But I wish she weren't here. We have to wait until she goes to bed. I see her with different eyes. Sneaky, mousy old Lucy, almost a spy. But this is Mother's decision. Even on our honeymoon, Mother would not leave me alone with a man.

The bride's veil must always be drawn over the union of two virgins, or should be. There is awkwardness from the strange moment of undressing — and perhaps seeing an adult male or female naked for the first time, the hesitancy and clumsiness, searching, sensing, finding, with no knowledge of foreplay — draw the veil! The suspense is intensely private and time passes.

Someone once said, "The fate of the house lies in the wedding night." At some point, several hours later, I wake to find Alec gone from our too-short double antique spool bed. I search. In my old room of childhood he lies, heaving with great and horrible sobs. I've never seen or heard a man cry before. Inarticulate, he can give me no clue as to what's wrong with me or him. I hold him close and finally lead him back to the double bed and with my arms around him, he sleeps again. New vows are made now and the fate of the house is sealed. As I go into the Robey world, I swear I will never willingly or unwittingly give him pain. The sharpness of a woman's tongue in potential devaluation or anger is now forever sealed off.

My eyes are wide open to the night, to the salt smell I love so, to the lap of waves almost below our window. I look over this first lesson in being a wife. And I sense dimly that although we are to be always together I am to be forever alone. I feel the first weight of the burden of the valley of wisdom and I know now that an altar, while it is for sacrifice, is also for suffering and a candle in silent prayer and a pledge. Is he a stranger, this man of mine? Why does he cry?

Mentally I leave the sea and look back at my country home I have now left for good. It sprawls into the fields, no other house near except for Uncle Tom's across the dirt road. Air and sun stream through the floor-length windows which Mother insisted upon when she renovated and enlarged the old farmhouse. Curtains are never drawn an inch. The house flows into the garden, the garden into the hayfields, and the fields, situated as they are on a hillside spur, reach out into the horizon and meet the sky on three sides. Furniture is a mixture of very antique and Victorian, Darby and Joan hang in the dining room, apple wood with its white ash and sweet smell is always burning in the fireplace, and family portraits look down over open bookshelves. I've never heard a cross word between my parents or known of illegitimacy or divorce or any other evil, gossip being strictly banned. The very air is clean and pure. And that early voluminous reading of fairy stories imprinted me with a certainty that when my prince did come we would marry and live happily ever after, even as did my parents and grandparents. Yet in the receiving line, so few hours ago, a horrid little thing happened. One of the first guests said, "It's a pleasure to meet you, Mrs. Robey."

"Who? Me?" Oh, no! I could have thrown my head back and given a long, terrible, mournful howl — a bitch of a howl. Am I a changeling? From maiden to matron and wife and now a mother to my Alec. A Robey for life. Oh, Alec, Alec, how can I save you from pain? A hurt little boy or frightened of something. I can become a true woman at her best — the perfect wife. Goodbye to the protective and placid ways of my Stevens family with its quiet containment, order, restraint, and great modesty of living. All will be changed now. I am entering a demanding and exciting world.

The Robeys own a large town house on Commonwealth Avenue. Their furniture is rich mahogany, turn-of-the-century Irving and Casson; the walls are adorned with large brown-framed photographs of such subjects as the Coliseum, the Discus Thrower, the Parthenon, and Michelangelo's David. Lights have to be on in the daytime everywhere except by the windows in the back room with a southern exposure. The first-floor parlor is full of beautiful leather-bound books — protected by locked glass doors. The shades are drawn down to mid-window, the velvet draperies partway across, and the view from the front is of the Mall and its elms. In back, across the alley, is an old brick elementary school and the children shriek throughout each recess. I am fascinated by the static solemnity and deep dim quiet.

I feel Alec's warmth and strength even through his sleep, and I become intimate with his clean body smell. I'm still bursting with adoration and gratitude at becoming a member of the

House of Robey. Mentally I study him. Six feet three, very erect, long-legged, slim and dark-haired, strong-jawed with a crooked smile and a little lift to the left corner of his mouth that gives a devilish look, two long scars from hairline to jaw because high forceps were used when he was born. He stutters some. He is as strong and powerful as Samson before his haircut. And the muscles and veins stand out like one of Michelangelo's athletes. He is a mighty, tender, and poetic man and he loves his mother deeply.

Why did he sob? Is he a frightened child?

We've touched base with my family to decide what wedding presents should be returned, and have seen the Robeys, just for a meal. Now we're in a New York room the day before the boat sails. I'm tired and want a nap, Alec wants a haircut. So I won't have to get up and unlock the door when he returns, he locks it from the outside with the big key. Soon there is a knock. "Who is it?"

"Flowers for you."

"But I can't unlock the door, he has the key."

Then comes a man's voice and a female voice which giggles and says, "He's locked her in already." I am annoyed. No one is going to lock me in without my permission.

We have fun aboard and fun abroad. I have learned now every step of a man's personal physical life. Alec shaves with a safety razor. (I am disappointed. I could remember so well being wakened by hearing through the wall between my bed and Father's bathroom his morning shave and I would go in and watch. There was the sound of steel on strop, whish, whish, flick, flack. Father had a fine set of seven blades in a case, one for each day. The bowl of soap, the beaver-hair brush wet from the basin of hot water, and flicked back and forth on the wooden soap bowl to make a fine, rich creamy lather; this then applied all over his face — he knew just how far hair extended. Now the razor, tested gently with thumb, and now drawn in clean, careful strokes down, across, around, to be wiped off on toilet paper, the little black hairs making fleas in the white suds. Then, finished, he washed his face clean of soap, holding the hot washcloth flat across his face for the moment in enjoyment. And everything was put away in order, the long razor wiped ever so carefully and folded into its handle and slid into the case pocket. It was then I would go and get in bed with Mother and snuggle up to her warmth.) I know now how a man buttons his fly, folds his clothes, and blows his nose, looking into his handkerchief as if a mouse might jump out. I know everything must be just so for him and that he gets anxious if anything is out of place. He teaches me all the four-letter words and tells me naughty stories. But he has to explain them all as I don't yet think sex is funny. He regrets that my breasts are so small. I think of his mother's large ones.

The whole honeymoon is all too comfortable and perfect to be memorable, but two pieces of art have clutched at my insides. Michelangelo's Pietà (Mrs. Robey and Alec?) and the Mona Lisa, which repels as well as mystifies me. I do not like that face. It scares me.

CHAPTER 3

The First Second Thoughts

OME AGAIN! We visit the Robeys on the Connecticut shore for a week before Alec starts work in my family's mill. So now I am a true daughter in the Robey dynasty and Mrs. Robey and I are so fond of each other. It should be fun to have her show me off to her summer friends. I suggest that I call Dr. and Mrs. Robey "Padre" and "Madre." They are pleased with this continental touch.

The first night, as a treat for me, I gather, there are steamed clams. A shiny new oilcloth that reeks of — oilcloth — covers the dining-room table. I comment that we didn't bother with this at home. We didn't seem to spill. Madre said, "Somebody will!" And as if under orders, my elbow hits the soup plate . . . it tips . . . clam juice spreads over the table.

"Ha!" Mrs. Robey shouts in a kind of joy, and belittling words pour out. They attack my know-it-all personality, and Alec sides with her, repeating her words almost verbatim. How *could* he? Dr. Robey, generally silent, looks troubled and alternately watches his wife's face, then mine.

Later, searching for comfort, I recall to Alec the wonderfully tender and sensitive quality of his love letters. He is pleased. "I got it all from *Bartlett's Familiar Quotations* and *The Oxford Book of English Verse*. I took what suited." I stare at him.

The next day Madre speaks seriously to me about how bad Alexander looks, drawn and worn out. She suggests ever so delicately but insinuatingly that my sexual demands are too much for him. I feel another flick of the adder's tongue. Again comes my cry of, "Why, why did she say that?" For I am hurt to the quick. How could she — there seem to be suggestions of sex in everything. Or do I hear it in everything? But I merely serve and do not initiate. I had been raised with Victorian denial of sexuality. One's duty is never to refuse one's husband no matter what or how you feel.

That night in the double bed overlooking the Sound, the door having closed us in to each other, the salt breeze blowing through the two wide windows, Alec wants me, as so often, and I wonder whether to listen to Mother or Madre. I ask myself again, why, for a woman, there is no physical pleasure while satisfying the male needs. And I hear Mother's voice saying again, "You must . . ."

He sleeps now, snoring softly. A dreadful realization staggers me. All passion gone! I don't love him at all! He's just a man and a fairly arrogant one. Now the lift to the left side of his lip seems sadistic. No, oh no! I look inward and outward at the night and can't see. I slip out and lie on the bed in the other guest room. Passion? What have I been, mad? What am I now? A dim and flickering light. But don't anyone ever be sorry for me. That's my department of personal pride. So love is dead, but not marriage. I promised to cleave and obey forever. Life is grief and sorrow and I'm too little. What is marriage? I vowed I would never hurt him. Oh, Mother, Mother, why didn't you tell me that marriage holds pain? Or maybe it never grieved you, you and Father so clean and simple, so fully, if shyly loving, so generous in spirit. And Mrs. Robey's sister, Anna, when I met her, said, "Be kind to Isabelle. I've got to warn you that she can be very difficult." I'd forgotten she said that. Why don't educators, clergy, the law, parents tell you of the emotional horrors to come?

Oh, pity, pity, I've been totally blind, deluding myself so deeply that the marriage had to be. Blind in my passion, now the blinders gone. Grief, guilt, and the shadow of that passion stirs my anger now. I look back and retrace. Everything holds a question mark.

Why did Mother push our engagement?

Each time Alec spent the night in the house last winter, and we sat in the little study before the fire and talked, each time when I went to bed, Mother was lying in it "to keep it warm" for me.

"Did you have a nice evening?"

And one of those nights in mid-March I whispered in awe, "He kissed me." My first kiss ever. She felt my voice. She always feels my voice. She held me tight for a moment and left.

"Sleep fast."

I did sleep hard and late, coming down at eleven. She said she was so happy for me, and Father was coming home to congratulate me on our engagement. He did, bringing a bouquet of flowers; his wishes were shy and tender. Alec and I were both dazed and impotent. Later Mother tackled him about his ability to make me happy. What else I don't know, but Alec emerged shaken. And Father talked to him that evening. So he never proposed to me. The engagement was announced two weeks later at a large reception at the Robeys' in the city. I had to wear a long dress. Oh, Mother, darling Mother, with your denial of sex and the impulses in yourself that therefore must be in me, did you not trust me? Or your training?

I had various beaux, several of whom proposed marriage. The girls called them "scalps in our belts" and I remember one very ardent suitor who had asked me to marry him over and over again. My response was merely respect and mild affection.

He was a gentle, rather passive scientist, mild, like Father. One bright full-moon night we were sitting — somewhere — and he said, "Would you at least let me hold your hand for a moment?" "For one minute," and I studied my watch by moonlight, my hand lying limply in his. "Time's up," and I withdrew it. No, there was only fear in me and my unconscious. How kind and patient he was. How cruel I could be. But I was far from ready even for that and hadn't Mother said, "Don't ever let anyone touch you"? And there was the, "If you are sitting on the ground, keep your legs crossed."

Why would Mrs. Robey let me see Alec so rarely between engagement and wedding? "You must study hard and graduate from Harvard Business School with high marks," she said to Alec. "You must not be emotionally stirred up."

But one weekend he did come and I met him at the train. He drove the car home and into the garage, and there in privacy he hugged me so hard, pressing against the middle of my back, that I fainted dead away. I vaguely felt him lifting me and saying sharply, "Stand up, stand up! Your father's coming." And as Father's car drove in beside us, I took Alec's arm and smiled a half smile. When later I told Alec he mustn't be so strong again he said, "I was told about that trick at college and it really works." On me? Why?

And those letters of Alec's that held so much beauty for me, and are now just the ashes of lies, why did he do that? And why did I have diarrhea from the time of our engagement until the wedding? Hadn't my younger brother told me seriously, "He'll break your heart the way he has with other girls. He's got a bad reputation"? I felt he was just being mean. And why did Father give Alec that stiff drink? Do men need it to stick together in an emergency? Why did Mrs. Robey take the wedding details away from Mother? Why did Uncle Tom get sick at this time?

And why, oh why, on my wedding eve, did Mother so lovingly, solemnly, and tenderly shave off all my pubic hair with Father's long, flat, sharp straight razor? What for?

"Your grandmother did it to me and it's what one does to be clean and sweet for the wedding." I shrank in horror and shame as I looked at myself in the mirror, shame and a sense of utter degradation. Never again would I look on little girls' bodies without discomfort. Alec was horrified when on our wedding night we turned, nude, to face each other.

In my disillusionment I see the whole wedding ceremony in another frame. It was a marriage hearse Father and I arrived in, and we moved down the aisle with slow dirgelike steps to the hymeneal music. (Hymen, the great god of marriage, my hymen, the end of youth and innocence, and those prurient Victorian faces staring. Exposed! Tonight! Tonight! As I stood beside Alec at the altar, the aeon-long commitment of woman to servitude was about to begin. And Alec was suddenly a given unknown.)

The two ministers benignly whittled their tongues for matrimony. *Dearly beloved, we are gathered together here in the sight of God and in the face of this company* . . . I shuddered. I could feel those faces behind my back in the big church. "Note this, all of you, I am being publicly sold." Of course, it was a nice suitable wedding in good taste but make your own evaluation as to the cost. Cry over the ceremony, you women, in terms of your own honeymoon night and your marital misery. Drool, you men, at the sight of my slim purity ready to be possessed. Long, you bridesmaids and ushers, for social-sexual weddings yourselves and wonder who will catch the bouquet.

To join together this man and this woman . . . Yes, I must be yoked, linked, shackled, hooked, harnessed, hobbled, and I would learn to be utterly beholden except in that secret withdrawn time of pregnancy where part of me would be emotionally *in camera.* . . . *holy matrimony instituted of God, in the time of man's innocence . . .* What God? Whose God? On what authority did he institute? Couldn't the law alone be responsible? And when were man and woman ever innocent? *Not to be entered into lightly . . .* Right! Incandescent bride-mind, brilliant with fear and anxiety, was my state. What about Alec's? *But reverently, discreetly, advisedly . . .* Wasn't passion always inadvised? *Soberly, and in the fear of God . . .* Sober, cold, frozen, in fear of life, yes. I was too naive to be in fear of God. I was merely terrified of myself. Dimly I saw ahead. Passion-crazy with an abstract idealized passion. Drunk with my first ecstasy, "quiet as a nun, breathless with adoration." No, not advisedly, we hadn't known each other well enough. Was it only a dozen times or fewer that we had ever been alone together learning love? Letters had to substitute.

Bitterness increases with each step of recall of the wedding rites. *If any man can show just cause why they . . . or else hereafter forever hold his peace.* That split-second suspension of breath throughout the church! Speak! Speak! Somebody cry out and save me from myself, from him. But nobody does ever speak out except in melodramas. They should have. They should have said, "Here is just cause. Their personalities don't fit. They aren't ready. He's a stranger and she's marrying in her first passionate reaching out, her first genuine open feelings. No way could a minister's pronouncement make her able to be one in physical flesh. Speak out! Tell her to wait, wait!"

The voice flowed on. *I require and charge you both, as ye will answer at the dreadful day of judgment when the secrets of all hearts shall be disclosed . . .* It's like some curse upon us. Oh, mea culpa, mea culpa, mea maxima culpa! For I was the original sin child. I must have been. Don't diminish and crush me so, you Dr. Gordon. Was it then that I winked in some sudden act of bravado or in defiance of the day of judgment? *That if either of you know any impediment why ye may not be lawfully joined . . .* That poor spooner-minister who said "joyfully loined" and ever

22

after hesitated before he came to those words, . . . *ye do now confess it.* How could we have confessed what we didn't consciously know about ourselves or what we could not visualize in the face of emotional impediments ahead? How could we be "joyfully loined" when not so long ago I was terrified to have a man's hand on my knee even cursorily, and only Alec's dominance and overwhelming love in his beautiful cheating letters made me able to accept his touch! Nature knows no pity when one is blind.

Will thou have this man to thy wedded husband? I would obey and serve him, love him, comfort him, honor and keep him, for I was brought up to love and obey my parents. *In sickness and in health, forsaking all others so long as ye both shall live?* Forsaking all others! Forsaking all others? Alec adores and is tied to his mother. I to mine. When I was born, I was given a name, which gave me an identity within my family and the community, though it was a few years before I stood off and looked at myself and said, "I am what I am, Harriet." The name, Harriet Lyman, had been held by many female forebears, thereby giving my identity double indemnity. My surname Stevens settled me into safety of the homeplace. I was one of a family and of a clan and of a tradition and a culture and a country. That was enough. And for almost twenty-three years, I listened and learned and obeyed. No longer an identity. No me. Oh, woe and despair. I was now a Robey. Mother, Father, safety of home, brothers, sisters, gone — gone forever. Obey and serve. I will obey and serve. I'm used to that. I will *try* to obey Alec in all things. He, the unknown, is now my lord and master, equal to my tenuous picture of God. Do I trust?

Who giveth this woman to be . . . Father, oh Father, don't give me away, for my heart has told me you aren't happy over Alec and you know I won't be happy because I should be marrying someone like you, mild and gentle and reasonable, not tough and assured like Alec and his mother. For the moment, given

23

but not yet taken, until Father said so softly, "I do." I was a thing given, a pawn. Or had he given me up?

I, Harriet, take thee, Alexander, to my wedded husband, to have and to hold . . . Through all the damnation that life metes out to us, or your mother metes out to me. *Till death . . . I pledge thee my troth.* I swore it and and instinct told me that I would be hurt.

Denying all others . . . I had never been denied. I hadn't yet found out what it was to deny myself. The Lord God had said that the man must cleave. The definition of *cleave*: to pierce or separate, especially along a natural line or division; to adhere, cling or stick by; to be faithful. As simple as that.

With this ring I thee wed. I am bound now. This is the circle of gold that shackles me. It is never to come off (except when I lay it aside to remind myself of something). *With all my worldly goods I thee endow* . . . Alec said that, I didn't. In this ceremony, women aren't supposed to own. If they do, it becomes their husband's automatically. All I have are a few accumulated favorite books, a revolver, *and* a canoe.

A vow and a covenant between us made. *In the name of the Father and of the Son and of the Holy Ghost. Amen.* This is a man's world. Where is Mary, why not "in the name of Mary who suffered as woman"? Is she the Holy Ghost? Or the mother of God?

Those whom God has joined together let no man put asunder. No man, but what about woman? Or snakes, or apples? Women are the servants and the chattels and a woman becomes a temptress when she's tired of being a thing, a servant.

I pronounce thee man and wife. He, the man, I the possession. Why not husband and wife or woman and husband? Love, honor, and obey! So why not use the word "trust" too? No one mentions trust. And does anyone ever say "the groom and bride"? No, this is her day. He is just a stud.

Is there any marriage where there isn't some memory of a

sexual relationship? It can lie like a stain on the purity of the ritual as ordained by the church. Now, finally, we were blessed by the ministers, as one flesh.

The ceremony was over. Bitter, bitter, I still understand nothing, and as the baa-blat of waking sheep on the hillside begins, I smooth the bed and slip back beside Alec again, still bewildered.

The next night I hold him close and whisper, "A child, give me a child, *please*, a child." For Alec holds the contraceptive power as provided by his father, Mother and I being in ignorance of such things. I have already found that Alec would, in his love, refuse me nothing. How am I to know that he wants no children at all, he wants only me?

My body responds to him wildly, joyously, and completely. As if, in fulfilling my woman's primal role and only then, could I break through the chains of sexual distaste that I was taught. A different tenderness for Alec fills me now. We will pick up our new life together and start our homemaking, leaving Madre to be the Queen Bee in this literate community, and to enjoy her coterie of admirers.

I ignore the questions, but they remain.

CHAPTER 4

The First Pregnancy and Isabelle

BOSTON NOW, Commonwealth Avenue, awaiting birth. I sit in the chintz-padded, wide-bottomed rocking chair in the sunny third-floor back guest room. The windows are open and gritty city air comes in. I'm waiting for the body within my body to send a signal, to take the first initiative. It's been a slow ten days.

My chief pleasure each day is a long, hot soak before bed. The tub is old-fashioned, very long, wide, and deep, and I'm in a dream state. With my body fully relaxed, my baby becomes active. The smooth protruding abdomen makes its involuntary motions — a bulge here, a heave or a jerk there, as if the fetus was crying to be let out.

Everything is ready: Dr. Huntington, the best obstetrician; Dr. Smith, the best pediatrician; a Phillips House private room; Miss Heartz, a trained nurse, engaged for six weeks. Father will drive Mother into the city day or night as soon as we notify them that labor has begun. (It is our family custom for the mother to be beside a daughter when her first child comes.)

Alec commutes to the city every night. Madre is being quite kind and very concerned. And as she worries that labor might start with only the maids, Margaret and Katy, there, she seldom goes out and often sits with me. She doesn't approve of very pregnant women being seen in public. She's been more sharing than at any other time before. Throughout the past "bridal" year, we've seen each other constantly. For Madre has been indoctrinating me — museums, morning musicals, concerts, contract and then duplicate bridge lessons — and every conversation was a lesson.

The Robeys have presented us with a pair of Saturday night Symphony seats. That means we must come in Saturday afternoon and stay the night, attending church the next morning so that we might be inspired by George Angier Gordon. Alec is still an usher in his cutaway, passing the plate with great dignity. Puss Leaman is practically always there. Only after a heavy roast lunch can we go home to Tewksbury. It's been a fun year building our nest with some furniture and equipment left by Uncle Tom, some from Mother's attic, a great mahogany dining set — solid Irving and Casson, the Robeys' wedding present. (Madre was going to give us a pair of beds but changed her mind when I said we wanted a double bed.)

One day Alec came home with a hammer and nails, wire cutters and wire and molding hooks. He didn't know quite how to start hanging pictures until I stood beside the stepladder and handed him the tools. His courage grew and this was the beginning of more and more facility which meant more and more tools. I for my part, isolated as we were in the country with no girl or women friends, went across the road to ask Mother's advice . . . housekeeping, sewing, cooking. A bride has so much to learn.

The Symphony has been my nemesis, but we must use that great gift. I have no ear for music, no interest in music, no training in music. As I sit in Symphony Hall my legs twitch and jump and go crazy. (The pregnancy, of course.) I pass the time in misery that is almost agony, finding no way to relax. So every Saturday night I count the bald heads, the white heads, the marcelled heads. I count the different colors of clothes, the seats, the lightbulbs. I reread the program and then turn it upside down to see if I can read it that way. What a waste of a seat that seems so important. Alec feels the same way about a woman singing. He has told me how Madre, who is proud of her voice and her playing, made him, as a small child, sit on the piano stool beside her — a preparation for the time when he would be old enough to go to Symphony. At five his own music lessons began. We have a radio now and whenever a woman's voice rises he snaps the controls off angrily.

Back in the fall Madre invited us to one of her choice dinner parties for twelve, perfectly appointed and served, exactly from seven to ten. No liquor offered. The next morning she gave me hell. "As Alexander's wife you've got — *got* — to learn to be a charming and intellectual dinner partner. Last night you looked absolutely stupid." I am sure Madre was right, and probably I've been overprotected and spoiled. But this was the first time I had ever been directly attacked. It still hurts me to think about it.

I sit and rock in the sun, knitting. Madre tells me the gory details about Alec's birth, how she was in labor for fifty hours and the baby would not come out. She was dying, almost dead, and the doctors made her drink very hot, very black coffee. She revived while they took Alexander by high forceps. She was informed that she must never conceive again.

With those long red cheek scars and large jaw, Alexander was so hideous she couldn't look at him. Nana was hired at once to take entire care of the child except for the midnight bottle, which Dr. Robey warmed and fed to the baby. Madre was proud of the fact that she couldn't stand the infant. But when the scars healed and then began to fade, she looked again. She saw that what she had was bonny. From then on she doted on her child, adoring him, knowing that he would be a great man. She signed her letters to Alec, C.S. I ask her what the C.S. stands for. Alexander was just talking a few words when she said one day, "You cunning thing!" and he came back with, "You cunny sing!" So that was who she was when she communicated with her son. Her letters, again unless she was angry, addressed him as "Monk" or "Cunck."

Her story makes me feel bad, sad, and uncomfortable. I sympathize. High forceps sound awful. But part of me hears something else. "How tough to be a woman." And yet I am looking forward, whatever comes, with a certain joy. Did she tell me the story to scare me or do I have a nasty, suspicious mind? This house, which a year ago was so dignified, elegant, rich, and velvety — even to the Oriental rugs — so enchanting in its dimness, luxury, and silence, now seems a dark, maligant place. Why else are glass curtains totally covering all windows? Why else are shades drawn halfway down with the velvet drapes drawn halfway across, turning light into a dim caricature of day? I mistrust. Are they afraid of anyone looking in? Or of themselves if they look out?

Madre believes in calling a spade a spade. She's proud of her mental honesty and clear-headedness, proud of her profound statements. She should have been a man. Padre, in one of our rare moments alone together, gave me a hug, a long kiss, and, speaking tenderly, said he was deeply thankful Alexander had gotten a warm, gentle, and understanding wife. The deep meaning in his voice spoke to me.

I know the hour by the sudden outburst of children's shouts and yells below my window. They are free. I am captive. I am trying to learn how to cope with it all. Just last week, at Sunday lunch, Madre burst out with some strong criticism of me and my family. It stung me. Alec repeated exactly her words, and then Padre, my only ally, took it up. I couldn't believe it. I couldn't take it. I jumped from my seat, ran as well as I could up the two long flights to my chintzy bedroom, locked the door, and lay on the bed sobbing. One by one the Robeys came up and knocked on my door. They wanted to apologize, but I was still crying so hard that I couldn't — or wouldn't — answer.

There are two of me. One could accept the apologies and comfort but compliance wasn't in me. The other "me" heard Keats's "Ode to a Nightingale": "Perhaps the self-same song that found a path/Through the sad heart of Ruth, when, sick for home,/She stood in tears amid the alien corn." Finally I was free of myself. They hadn't killed me. I was me and this was my baby. We were one.

Time passes. But so slowly. I sit in the bedroom studying the chintz curtains with their roses, the same chintz bedspreads, the trellised roses of the wallpaper which climb stiffly to the high ceiling. My heart leaps as I hear the shrieks of freedom across the alley. I can set my watch by that clanging bell and those yells. All the children can do is play in a small asphalt and wire-fenced square, boys on my side of the building, girls on the other. At least they scream. Oh, Alec, Alec, what and where have I missed? Perhaps — though I won't admit it — I'm afraid.

At every chance I pin Madre down to family history. She is reluctant to tell anything, as if there is some closet skeleton. She gives me only the stark details. I realize suddenly that there are no words of feelings, no descriptions, no incidents, except for one — her childish plaint, "Poppa eye me!" — which she repeated in real and rare amusement.

The eighteen-year-old Andrew Alexander immigrated to America from Sterling, Scotland, in 1853, unknown but determined, with the proverbial fifty cents in his pocket and a crest left somewhere behind. But he wore all the power of his stubborn Scotch Covenanter background, with John Knox, Luther, and Calvin and his literal belief in the Bible as his original wealth and strength. By the time he died, he had founded and made famous the Andrew Alexander Shoe Store on Fifth Avenue near the corner of Forty-second Street, filled the front pew in the Central Presbyterian Church, was settled into the Social Register, and was very wealthy. This took hewing to the conservative line, giving more than his tithe yearly, and acting with an authority so cold, stern, and righteous that he appears to have become a veritable Jehovah. He married gentle and apparently compliant Mathilda Torrens, and gave her six children, four of whom died young, leaving only the fourth and sixth, Anna and Isabelle. Isabelle was born when her mother was forty-two.

The household ran by his big watch, presumably turnip-size and solid gold. There were prayers for all the household every morning and no one could be missing; lights must all be out by ten o'clock; nothing could be cooked on Sundays though cold food was served. Only the Bible could be read on that day and church attendance must be thrice.

Where Anna was mild and obedient, Isabelle was a willful rebel. It was stubborn determination against her father that gained her a B.A. and M.A. at Hunter College. She was enrolled in the University Law School, having received a cash prize for the best entry exam, when she met and married the young Dr. William Henry Robey from Dorchester, Massachusetts, a Harvard Medical School graduate. Dr. Robey had set up practice in the ell of half a double house in Roxbury, the property including a stable for his horse and carriage. Roxbury was at that time a desirable suburb of Boston and to this home he would bring his bride. But when I pushed her a little too far on personal details she would answer, "I'm not interested."

Another day I try to find out about Dr. Robey's background. Did she seal his lips as she did her own? He obviously had no history. His father, with a partner, a Mr. French, owned the Robey/French Camera Store on Bromfield Street. He had a brother, but Madre did not care for the brother's wife as she was not "quite." Relations were so successfully broken off that they had never been mentioned in my hearing. I wonder if they were even invited to the wedding?

I find myself, as I rock, wait, and rock, in a sudden realization.

If Andrew Alexander achieved what he did in one generation, it must have been by doing everything correctly, socially and in business. Therefore, his daughter, emulating him, worked hard to reach the social heights of Boston through constant attention to etiquette, although she never achieved the Chilton Club. Like father, like daughter.

I have a sudden sour taste in my mouth, just as the rain starts spattering, making clean rivulets on the sooty pane. Madre approved the engagement because I had a face like a sheet of fine paper, ready to be drawn or etched upon or lined in any way she saw fit. She could mold me as she molded Alec.

I can imagine old Andrew Alexander like the Lord when he said unto Moses, "I have seen this people, and behold, it *is* a stiff-necked people: now therefore let me alone, that my wrath may wax hot against them, and that I may consume them . . ." Had not Madre inherited this also?

I'm getting a suspicious feeling about Madre's values and goals. You don't become somebody unless you are distinctive and original, yet always in perfect taste, demanding and getting the best. Bitter, bitter must I have become to her. Did she not feel Alexander pulling away from her?

I still have Madre captive in a way. "Tell me about Puss Leaman?" I ask.

"He was Hal's best friend in high school but didn't go on to college. He's brilliant in financial matters and became a partner in his brokerage house when quite young. He's always been the family's closest friend and my financial adviser since my father died."

I think back before the wedding to the little dinner Mr. Leaman gave us in his apartment on Beacon Hill. Mother and Father and the Robeys were also there. He owned the whole building and rented out floors, reserving the ground level for his own fine dining room, where Steer, the caretaker, cooked and served. Mr. Leaman was very impressive. He had a limousine and an impeccable putteed chauffeur. He had a camp and guides on Lake Umbagog in Maine. He owned a colonial farmhouse in Hopkinton, Massachusetts, where he had everyone for Thanksgiving and other outings. That night after dinner, back in his apartment overlooking the lights of the city, I noticed the rows of beautifully shined shoes in his bathroom. I asked what polish he used. "My own urine," he said. "It gives a hard, lasting sheen." Was this another part of Boston I hadn't seen? He had such perfect clean linen, such immaculately pressed suits — always made by Dunne — such pink cheeks, such shiny white hair. Anyone would trust him, or want to. Probity stood out all over him: dignity, precision, rectitude, and total courtesy.

Andrew Alexander died in 1904, Mathilda a year later. Everything went to his two daughters, including the store and its location. Madre went on, "Anna's husband, Sam Murtland, wouldn't let any woman of his have anything to do with business. So I had to buy the store. We fought. We didn't speak for three years. Then we made up."

How sad. She and her only admitted relative. I see parents, children, and family loyalties in a new way. Inheritance, indoctrination, or obedience out of fear — life holds all the elements of tragedy. Do all marriages have one mate in subservient bondage to the other? This lovely, lonely rocking chair opens my mind and my ignorance shames me.

A bit more I am able to gather. Madre bought out Anna's share of the store. With her masterful mind challenged she could, of course, run it. She went to New York once a week but relied on the old, original manager, Mr. Bemis, for the day-to-day decisions. In the summer she rented a house in Stonington, Connecticut, from which she could go to New York for a day. With her inheritance, the Robeys moved from Roxbury to Commonwealth Avenue. In the process, I imagine she discarded much of her old furniture and bought a great deal of

Irving and Casson as well as heavy velvet hangings and more and better china and silver. She acquired a limousine and chauffeur and entered the social world fully. Dr. Robey could no longer be a general doctor — he became a heart and lung specialist, his private office on the ample fourth floor of their home. (Patients were hauled up in a creaky little elevator.) He eventually became full professor at the Harvard Medical School, teaching at Boston City Hospital.

Meanwhile, Alexander went to Rivers Country Day School, to dancing school, had riding lessons and weekly piano lessons, attended concerts and Symphony. In late adolescence he worked in a settlement house. He went to church every Sunday.

A woman must be proud to give birth well. Proud and strong inside. That night as I'm getting ready for bed the "water" breaks. I shout down to the living room and get dressed again. Phillips House is called, Dr. Huntington is called, Miss Heartz is called, and a cab is called. While waiting, I ask Alec if he has reached Mother to tell her to come. I need her. I need her love and support. My first child is being born. Madre suddenly yells out in rage. "Who do you think you are, making your mother and father come all the way into Boston this time of night? You're the most selfish, thoughtless, self-centered young woman I've ever seen. I always knew it. Alexander, I forbid you to call her. Don't you touch that phone. I forbid it." I cower. I cannot blurt out the beautiful, wildly awful words of fury that almost form, for I am looking at Alec's face. On it is sheer terror, not a loving obedience to his mother's will against his wife's. He is immobilized.

The doorbell rings — the taxi is here. Alec carries my bag, Padre sees me solicitously down the stairs, down the front steps, and into the cab.

34

CHAPTER 5

Confinement—The First Son

FOR THE FIRST time I'm in a hospital. My clothes are replaced by a wrong-way-round pajama top tied in the back. The nurse, capped, pinned, and rustling with starch, has left to report to Alec and Dr. Huntington that it will be four to six hours yet. And while she's gone, a volcano within me blows and almost blasts the baby out. Everything else in that violence lets go. The strawberry shortcake of dinner looks like blood. And I mess the bed with my stool. In the worst kind of terror, ashamed and disgraced.

I pray. I plead. I cry out to God.

God doesn't hear.

Again, my body agonizes. The nurse returns, rings the bell sharply, and spends the rest of the time bracing and pushing the emerging baby's head back each time a labor contraction forces it out again. It's her strong arms against my whole limber but unathletic body fighting her by instinct for the life force.

The bed is jolted into the elevator, jolted off. The ether cone settles on my face. When I am aware again, I wonder what that extraordinarily swift delivery means. Either I am a very primitive woman or a very angry one. It never occurs to me that it might mean something else.

But now I know what it means to give an heir to the House

of Robey. The baby is named after Mrs. Robey's father (and incidentally after my husband), and I find myself to be in full favor. Special delicacies of food are brought in daily by Mrs. Robey — lobster Newburg, pâtés, meringues with strawberries, and squabs — all the goodies she knows I like. Presents and flowers come from her friends and my relatives. I lie in bed against a pink lace and silk pillow sham and under a matching bedspread Mrs. Robey has given me.

I'm half ashamed of myself when I ask Miss Heartz to wheel me to the sunporch but I need fresh air. I adorn myself a little more by holding a long-stemmed rose in one hand, resting the other hand on the gold-green leather and onionskin paper *Oxford Book of English Verse*, Alec's first present and an ever-ready solace in time of need. A pink velvet ribbon is in my hair, my bedjacket is rose, and the lacy nightgown underneath is pink. I am a princess again. There aren't many people in the hall, but they look at me.

As for little Andrew — at once called Sandy — his mouth and my nipples do not draw together by instinct and inspiration. He fumbles at the suddenly hardened nipple, which hurts and will not give him the great soft mouthful to suck. He's put on a bottle quickly. The authorities are relieved. They have advised against nursing all along: a bottle is much healthier. I feel little love for the child, but I am intensely, maternally protective of him.

I find that having the best specialists (which means the latest knowledge) dictates my day. For fear my "heavy uterus" may fall, I cannot get out of bed. I dangle my legs over the side on the sixteenth day, stand briefly the seventeenth, go to the bathroom once on the eighteenth. My baby is brought to me once a day — all fresh and sweet and dressed up, for me to hold or feed by bottle. At about three weeks I will be ready to go home, my nurse with me, at which point I'll be allowed to go downstairs once a day — for another week. The nurse will leave at the end of six weeks and I'll be free, in a manner of speaking.

About the fourth day in the hospital I am tensing up with the need for motion. I can stand on my head strongly and steadily, so one day when Miss Heartz is out of the room I do so on the bed. She comes back, shrieks, and gives me hell. "But you said the uterus would drop if I was on my feet. How could it if I was upside down?"

"You'll get an embolism and maybe die," she snaps. That silences me. Another impulsive act, another sin. Everything I do seems to be wrong. All Mrs. Robey's food, adoration, presents, and flowers cannot make up for that moment of her utter bitterness and scorn at my selfishness in wanting my mother.

I'm home again. The six weeks are over. Miss Heartz has gone. But Mother is across the road. My legs are still weak from the long incarceration. Mrs. Robey arrives one day with Alec's old nurse, little Nana. She has not asked my permission. Of course her grandson should have his father's nurse — as if the baby were her own child. But lines aren't drawn yet. Nana is so gentle, so utterly happy, so busy about the baby that every little while she goes and feels lightly to see if he's wet or has drooled. She changes him at the slightest moisture or uses one of the fine linen guest towels to wipe his mouth. Then the offending cloth goes into the hamper. She has nothing else to do, and his clothes pile up, as does my frustration. I clean all the diapers she has dropped in the pail and wash all the towels and shirts and dresses in Uncle Tom's antiquated washer. There's no way I would or could ask her to help with the housework. Then one day I catch her tiptoeing to the bassinet that lay in the shade outside to change Sandy for the second time in fifteen minutes. I dare at last. I dare to tell Mrs. Robey that I don't want Nana around. I have to learn to take care of my own baby.

The next day I put the baby basket out on the lawn as usual. On going out to check on him, I hear rustling of the leaves in the basement window well a few feet away. I look in and see the biggest black snake ever. The snake's girth looks about the size of my little Sandy's neck. Horrible visions flash. With Sandy inside and safe, I take from a drawer the tiny blue-gray Colt revolver with its snub nose and nice palm-fitting capacity. Uncle Tom had given it to me because I wanted to be dramatic and have a revolver at my belt when I rode alone along the country roads. Standing now over the window well, scared and determined, I fire two shots at the snake in the leaves. He ceases writhing and I draw him out with a rake. Heavy indeed he is! And by measurement he is five and a half feet long. Is this cold, merciless, premeditated murder?

My Sandy sleeps in the guest room across a large hall from our room and bath. Alec doesn't like to hear babies cry. But my mother's reproaches go far deeper than Mrs. Robey's. "I heard Sandy crying for two hours straight last night. You'll *have* to have him nearer you." I'm horrified at my neglect. Then one day Alec tells me we must move. He says I am much too dependent on my mother, asking her questions about everything. "You're too close to her." I want to say, "What about you and your mother?" But I hold my tongue.

Sandy is thriving now. It's been a bad three months of colic. A change of formula helps. Dr. Smith absolutely forbids picking up a baby before four hours are up, and Sandy has three-hour hunger. "Crying exercises his lungs. You may play with him for ten minutes just before his next feeding." But by four hours I have been pacing, my fingers, arms, and brain aching, and the baby is too exhausted from screaming to take the bottle when the time comes. It is agony for both of us.

In the fall Mrs. Robey begins "borrowing" Sandy. She has bought a crib, high chair, bottle sterilizer — everything. It would be cruel to say "no." Nana now cares for him sedulously at the Robeys.

One evening Alec comes home cold and sick-looking. "She's withdrawn her yearly allowance and is changing her will. She's leaving everything to the YWCA," he tells me. "She doesn't approve of our lives." I hug him. What else is there to do?

We now start house-hunting, and are pleased with a simple late-Victorian house in a fairly good neighborhood, just like so many other houses — little, ordinary, and cozy for us. But Mother takes one look and declares that is not good enough for us. I hadn't seen that snobbery before. She busies herself, buys a granite "castle" and stable, makes the stable over for us, and fixes five apartments in the "castle." Mother's at her happiest remodeling anything.

There seems to be repressed sexuality in me, in Mother, even in Mrs. Robey. One day I had taken Sandy in to Boston and on leaving, said to Nana, "Don't forget to pull back his foreskin when you wash him." Mrs. Robey almost screamed, "Don't you ever use that word in this house again!" Another time she told me of one of her highly esteemed Boston friends with three married sons in business in the city. They come back each night to see how she is because this is what sons should do with their mothers. But she also makes them tell her whether they have had relations with their wives the night before and as Mrs. Robey said, "I think that's going a bit too far."

I'm seven months pregnant again when we move into our new stable-house. Most attractive and unusual. One of Mrs. Robey's bitter letters arrives for Alec. As usual it diminishes even his shadow. Certainly it increases my guilt, for I feel in truth it is talking to me.

February 5, 1926

Dearest Cunck,

If you weren't precious to me beyond expression, I wouldn't feel as deeply as I do and as I have. You may have thought that

39

my disappointment today was out of proportion or lacking in understanding. I am depressed as has been the case so many times within the past year or two. The promise of your childhood and youth in the way of a response to beauty shows less and less signs of fulfillment.

Do you ever find time to look at yourself objectively? As your life appears to me now, your occupations and your general attitude are becoming thoroughly materialistic, self-centered and provincial — and your powers of receptivity to enlarging ideas steadily weakening. I see no evidence of growth within yourself. You have become so rigid at your age that you do the stupid, unintelligent thing of avoiding new music or new poetry.

"But what shall it profit a man if he gain the whole world and lose his soul?" For years you drew something of inspiration and some of exaltation occasionally from Dr. Gordon — now one more source of stimulus has been abandoned and you have sought nothing to take its place. If you have given up church connections entirely and have cut yourself off completely from your inherited and traditional training, what are you going to put in its place and what path are you going to set your children's feet upon?

I can and do sympathize with the mother who has had her children's interests as the one thing in life and who has had them shifted so that she can no longer be what she wants to them. It would be impossible for me now to bear not only the loss of contact and confidence, but the source of disappointment. But after all, you are still my beloved son and I must hope that I may at least occasionally say some of the things that are in my heart trusting that they will be given consideration.

Oh, think with life spread before you, don't give it all to Mammon so that the great forces that are about us can't work on your spirit, nor the roots of sweetness and aspiration which sprouted in your youth shrivel from lack of soil and nurture. After all that has been said, I love you more than you'll ever know.

Love, Mother

Of course, she was right in a way. We live different life-styles, chiefly based on my family example, which is not to be bound by conventions. We are newlywed creators, not feeding on others' creativity. In the new house I do murals or Italian designs on the great beams overhead. I make better and better use of my sewing machine. I practically invent cooking. We make lots of friends in Lowell. Alec performs miracles of invention and convenience in cabinetwork, constantly discovering new use of body and mind. He also finds he can act magnificently on the amateur stage. There he is another man, a completely free man, his motions spontaneous and true to the role and the drama that can be part of all of us. There is no time, as we innocents see it, for church, settlement work, or writhing over others' artistic creations.

To please Mrs. Robey I had tried visiting at the Tewksbury Insane Asylum where they also house the severely handicapped. Two young women were "mine." Alas — no supervision. I was thoroughly milked by the lies and the requests and the false flattery. I quit, not yet ready in my innocence for the sights, sounds, and needs of so many.

Yet Mrs. Robey's letter leaves me bewildered, angered, sad, very sorry, compassionate, and totally at a loss other than giving honest praise to Alec.

A few weeks later our second child is born two and a half weeks prematurely — in the car.

CHAPTER 6

The High-Speed Delivery and the Premie

WAKE about nine-thirty that cold April night with a contraction tightening me. But the baby isn't due! Another! I time them — one minute apart. I wake Alec, he dresses fast. I call Dr. Huntington — no answer. Alec calls his parents, just in from Symphony. "We're coming. We have Sandy with us." I put on my slip and underwear — the English imports, silk and wool with knee elastics. Then further warning comes — grab trousseau winter coat — fine gray broadcloth wool, squirrel collar and cuffs.

"Alec, take down the baby's bag and I'll bring Sandy. But hurry!" I put a blanket around fat little Sandy in his Dentons — he doesn't stir. Down two curving flights to the cellar garage. Suddenly a deeper bearing-down contraction. I grasp the banister and stand trying to balance Sandy and myself. When free, I continue down to the cellar, lay Sandy in the back seat of our wide two-door sedan, cover him, and get in beside Alec. He backs the car out.

Alec turns to me and says, "You forgot to turn out the light. Go shut it off."

But I'm scared and busy now. "To hell with the light — go to the Lowell General Hospital."

"I don't know where it is. We're paying for the best and you're going to get it."

"Please, there's not time." But I say it softly, feeling helpless.

We head for Boston — bumpy country roads first, then the highway. Really hard bearing-down contractions now that use all my body strength and I grunt as if I were hauling up a huge mainsail. There are no chanteys to help me. At each strain my body braces itself. Feet are out on the floor, head and shoulders on the back of the seat, body in between arched.

There are three deadly rips of pain which *are* pain . . . I suddenly relax. Hear a tiny kitten-sneeze. Then silence. "It's come!" I reach down into my bloomers and draw out the infant. "No rush now." We still have half an hour's drive ahead and Alec goes steadily, strongly and fast, but not crazily fast. He means business. He doesn't speak. I don't think of him. I unbutton my coat, lay the sticky, wet baby against my breast and button up again. I'm afraid of the exposure of the cold night air. Now it's safe against my heartbeat, my body warmth, my smell; in darkness, hearing the purr and feeling the motion of the car. How wonderful. I reach out to take Alec's hand and hold it, for I'm sitting in a heaven of incredible euphoria that fills me to overflowing. I quote fatuous poetry.

I suggest that we go through red lights, hoping a policeman might whistle and stop us, look in, jump on the running board and, shrilling his whistle, speed us on our way. But no, no policeman.

At the big steps of Phillips House, Alec, leaving the motor running, runs up into the lobby, comes back with Dr. Huntington. Now is my biggest, proudest moment. I hold the naked infant up to the window. Never was woman so proud, so joyful.

"Afterbirth come?"

"I wouldn't know."

To Alec, "Drive around to the ambulance entrance. I'll meet

you there." Alec tells me with comic relief that when he had announced the baby had already arrived, his mother half screamed, "It isn't done! Keep it secret." Dr. Robey stays with her to soothe her.

Dr. Huntington lifts me bodily, the baby rebuttoned into my coat, and lays me on a wheeled stretcher. Now I need not react to anything. Not unconscious, but utterly relaxed and remote beyond anything but us two, mother and child. We, one. In the delivery room, I cry out against the dreaded ether cone as it appears but am told there's more work to be done.

The next morning Dr. Huntington comes in, sits down pompously and, shaking his head sadly, says, "Terrible. Terrible. In a week or ten days when you're over the shock I'll ask you to give me the details. It must have been dreadful pain."

"I'll tell it now. It was a *wonderful* experience."

His expression refutes me. "The pain was terrible."

"It wasn't. Just the last brief tearing ones."

"My dear. There's always pain in childbirth. Every woman suffers terrible pain. I know."

"But I didn't. It was wonderful."

Again he shakes his head. "Women always endure terrible pain. Driving so fast must have acted like an anesthetic."

Now I am *angry*. He's taking my baby and my joy away from me. "Since I did half the work you should only charge half price. Five hundred dollars is an awful lot for us."

Alec sleeps well at his mother's after that drive. But the next night he has the jitters. He's been telling so many people to get release, but only gets more tense. I hear him once. "It was terrible! She screamed the entire twenty-five miles." I don't comment. Let him have *his* moment of glory. Mine is mine and must be secret since even the great Dr. Huntington won't believe me. However, his bill, when it came, was two hundred and fifty dollars.

I am no princess this time. Mrs. Robey proudly makes the

strong statement, "I had one father, I have one husband, one son, one grandson. Otherwise, I'm not interested."

She still claims Sandy periodically. He loves it, loves the attention and admiration he gets from Margaret, Katy, Nana, and his grandparents. One day I'm there when some friends come to call. Sandy, now two, is all dressed up in short pants, a perfect-fitting Eton jacket, wide starched collar, and a bow tie. He bows to the guests as she has taught him, with his right hand resting on his abdomen, his left hand against the small of his back, palm out, and his bow is as deep as his fat little belly will allow. I go out of the room feeling sick.

Mrs. Robey calls or writes every day, Alec visits her when in Boston on business. She gives him a new Mason and Hamlin baby grand so he can get back to his music. The tone is wonderful, they say. At another time she is very pleased to present us with a pair of pineapple maple beds, beautiful copies of antiques to replace our cheap, white-enameled iron one. I find the mattresses just exactly fit crosswise, each three feet three inches by six feet six inches. After a decent interval, Alec and I push them together. There may be no passion, but familiarity, smell, compassion, and the love of touch arises with affection. Flesh so compatible, minds so incompatible. One couple I know — he on the downward alcohol path, she improving herself and her children — had one old-fashioned double bed. She lay on her side, almost falling out, one arm down to the floor rigidly held there all night lest she turn in her sleep and touch him. She was all anger. He was hopeless.

I've taken to the flute, hoping by concentrating on one instrument I might better grasp the whole sound of the symphony and better endure those Saturday evenings. A few lessons with a local teacher, then my head swells. I'm taken on for lessons by George Laurent, first flautist of the Boston Symphony Orchestra. He lives on the fourth floor of a brick apartment building in the Fenway. No elevator. The enormity of my optimism strikes me hard one day, when I, pregnant again, can't catch my breath enough after the long climb to play a clean, pure note. Obviously M. Laurent is bored to death and I'm no pleasure to him beyond money. I myself know I am hopeless. Also I know I am ridiculous. Why do I ask for the best when I am the impossible worst? When my half hour is about up, I'm at last able to control my breathing. I quit, but I do play simple things with Alec accompanying me. I also learn to play on the piano, for the children, nursery songs from "The Baby's Bouquet" and "The Baby's Opera." But only the songs in the keys of C, F, and G. That's all I know.

It is spring of 1929 when Dr. Huntington induces labor two and a half weeks early. He must have had no taste for an incredibly swift birth. Doesn't his reputation come in here also? Tam is certainly premature — gavage feeding in the hospital, then slow, patient, teasing bottle feeding by Miss Heartz at home. He's like a picked chicken, bony and listless. Have I enough love for a third son? Isn't there always room enough for a son? He's a funny one. He neither walks nor talks until he is about fifteen months old. He sits on the floor, just sits, looking, listening, studying. His eyes shine with quick comprehension or are dreamy in concentration. No way could one call him retarded. He watches every happening around, especially with the other children, but without reacting. He has one most frustrating trick, repeated ad nauseam. Sitting there, with those skinny little baby fingers, he undoes the strong safety pin that holds the three points of the triangularly-folded diaper in place. Then whatever happens, happens, and I clean up.

In the stock-market crash we lose nothing because we have nothing to lose. The Robeys never mention their concerns. Mrs. Robey has the same secrecy about financial affairs as she does about her family.

But the crash presages anxiety and depression. Alec and I are having picayune troubles; he criticizes me as his mother does him. If I defend myself his anger rises to a frightening peak and I am beaten down, swearing never to cross him again. Sometimes when I am absent he is sadistic with the children. Sometimes he is kind. And I'm like a yo-yo going up and down in my personal depression.

The smallest differences are sometimes mountains. I cut the grass in great circles, never slowing my pace. He cuts the grass in absolutely straight lines, stopping at the end of each row, turning cleanly and walking back again. He squeezes toothpaste from the bottom of the tube, I from the middle. It drives him crazy. But my hand is much smaller than his and squeezes more accurately when I hold the tube in the middle. He lays the fire one way, I another. I've had years of experience with open fires, he's had almost none. And nothing irritates him more than a dripping faucet. Why doesn't he put in a new washer?

Oh, you damned "best" doctors. After Tam's birth and I'm settled at home again, I find Jock listless and playless. He sits in his room with my old 1904 fur-worn teddy bear, stroking it rhythmically, his eyes closed, his tongue sucking and clicking against the roof of his mouth. I check with Dr. Smith. "*That's* masturbation. Take the teddy away immediately." I do, with sorrow. Within a day or so Jock stutters so badly no words come out at all. Horrified, I give back the bear with an apology. It is three months before his speech is normal again.

Had I been more sensitive to Alec's needs, I wouldn't have asked for still another child. I am at my healthiest and steadiest when pregnant and though three boys are certainly enough, I feel some great primitive drive; a girl, a daughter, I must have to be complete. Alec should have a girl. I'd heard of a Dr. Swaim, a reputable gynecologist, who has a "recipe" for getting either a boy or a girl. I impetuously go to him, get his instructions, pay my seventy-five dollars, and press Alec, who as usual can refuse me nothing. We try once more.

I'm the balance wheel between four male personalities and

47

I want more? I want to have what my body tells me to have.

Within a few weeks, excitement catches on among all the Robeys. And Mrs. Robey begins: if it is a girl its name, of course, would be Isabelle. Through the months the pressure grows. Every time Alec visits his mother he comes back solemnly saying that we have to name a girl baby for her. Tension grows greater as the due date approaches. Poor Alec — that one last try of mine for the desperately wanted daughter and he caught between two women the whole nine months.

Instinctively I know that my mother-in-law — now Mrs. Robey to me, no longer Madre — and I are enemies and if I name a daughter Isabelle I would lose my child to her, my new and better self, and I might come to hate her.

The baby is induced (a full glass of castor oil — gagged down), labor begins two and a half weeks early as with Tam, anesthesia is given . . . from afar I hear a voice, "It's a girl, Mrs. Robey. Can you hear me? It's a girl." I feel some tears making their cool path down my cheeks. "A girl" — coming and going in my ether-befuddled brain. I feel myself wheeled into an elevator, out of an elevator, and into my room. Feel hands slide me from the stretcher to my own bed. I open my eyes. Dr. and Mrs. Robey and Alec all sit there waiting.

I am congratulated. As they leave, Dr. Robey kisses me. Mrs. Robey says, "How lovely! And of course it will be Isabelle, dear." And she pats me.

I am barely able to say thickly, "Wait, wait. I don't know yet. I don't know."

Alec leaves last. "It's *got* to be Isabelle. She'll never forgive or forget. It's the most important thing in her life; in my life."

Again I say, "I don't know yet." And I begin to cry.

CHAPTER 7

It's Harriet, and Isabelle Is Furious

$\mathcal{I}$T'S FOUR weeks later, four weeks of daily calls to Alec from his mother, four weeks of growing tension for him and for me, of his pleading each night until Miss Heartz says he can't even come into the room if he doesn't stop nagging me. The card for registration of birth and name has not yet gone to the authorities.

The Robeys are due for Sunday lunch tomorrow. Before he gets into bed Alec puts the paper and a pen beside my pillow. "You've *got* to settle it tonight. Isabelle! Isabelle!" Again I'm tangled in one of those wakeful nights, caught between duty to my husband, to his family and particularly to his proud mother, and the demand of my own nature. A long, long night of going over the pros and cons, the rights and wrongs. It's about five A.M. when I write firmly, "Harriet Lyman," a name passed down for at least the past five generations of loyal, decent, strong, and somewhat self-effacing women along with their funiture, their silver, and a family tradition. In the morning I hand Alec the card. He reads and goes very still. Nothing is said but I know he feels sick.

The Robeys arrive. We are all avoiding one subject. They check with the children and then we go in to lunch, cooked and served by my six-dollar-per-week state ward. Finally, just before desert, I explain that I have decided, that I know I am very selfish, that Alec wants the name Isabelle more than anything else, but that Harriet Lyman is too important a part of my family tradition and I am the only one who carries on the name. I'm terribly sorry but it has to be so. Harriet Lyman is the name.

Mrs. Robey stands up at once, saying, "Come, Hal!" She marches out of the room, through the hall, out the front door, and gets in the car without a word to either of us. Dr. Robey is driving. He looks back at me sadly. The car is gone now. I know that Alec is in some sort of shock. He rejects my touch. I'm terribly sad, yet I feel good.

In the following days and weeks Alec often telephones his mother and she always slams down the receiver. It is only after three months that some communication begins. She allows him to go and see her. What she says I'll never know, but he comes home deeply depressed. "She no longer calls you 'Hap.' She speaks of you as 'your wife.' "

Then I really laugh and hug him. "Don't you realize how many years it's been since I began referring to her as 'your mother'?" Light dawns slowly. Then he, too, laughs. At last he could laugh! And I see that some sort of peace has come to him. What he was grasping I don't know.

It is a year all told before Mrs. Robey sees or talks with me. She calls our daughter "Miss Robey." It is still not all joy. My anger has eroded, and I'm sorry for both the Robeys. We become cautiously comfortable. She's even begun to admire me. This makes it awkward. Was she ever crossed in her life before by a woman?

She pulls, however, one more attack. I'm out with the baby, the boys are in school, and she arrives at our home with her three closest women friends — no announcement, no permission. We always leave the door unlocked. She shows her guests all over, pointing out the things we've done to make it so unusual. That night she calls and asks directly for me. Uh-uh! The telephone sizzles with her rage. "In your bathroom the toilet was unflushed, filled with stool. A dirty mess. Before all my friends. How could you!"

I say that we naturally always flush the toilet but often one of the children uses our bathroom. "Impossible," she says, "the stools were much too large for a child." Of course it wasn't her son. Obviously, I was the culprit. Obviously, I was unclean. So what right had she to come and enter without asking first? Christ! It's not *her* house.

And now we are caught up in a maelstrom of depressions — the Great Depression and my own depression — never getting quite to the bottom, never being thrown out of the swirling eddy into calm.

CHAPTER 8

Depressions Strike

T'S SPRING of 1937. I've graduated to the rattan chaise longue on the porch of Mother's house in Ormond, Florida. I'm beginning to think again, feel again, know again. Depression has been deep, starting with the high fever; no, starting almost upon my arrival for my annual visit-vacation. In my childlike enthusiasm, I show Mother what a male neighbor and I have been lightheartedly writing about — men and women and marriage, and being as silly as possible.

Mother reads it. "It's not worthy of my lovely Harriet. It's cheap." I wake up the next morning with the fever. The local doctor and the one called from Winter Park can make nothing of it. Though the fever abates, the depression deepens to utter passivity. I can't move without great effort of will and sometimes there isn't any will.

Mother sits, sits, sits beside me. At times her face appears as the Mona Lisa — far too complicated to read, holding me back in the primitive darkness which contains inescapable horrors; other times by sheer will pulling me into health and reality. Leave me alone! Go away! Don't look at me like that! I have an eerie feeling she's working magic for good or mind-destroying evil with her patient, directed, loving intensity.

Alec has brought down the two youngest children to attend

a small private school here. The two oldest are boarding at the Fenn School in Concord, where they have been day pupils.

From Massachusetts, Alec calls to say Sandy had to have his appendix removed. Alone! And I not there to cradle his thirteen years in my love.

From the porch I watch the birds get drunk eating overripe palmetto berries. They totter, fall, stagger up, fall again. By and by they are gone. They are funny to watch, and are reminiscent of Prohibition episodes up north. I watch a rat run up the tall bare trunk of a huge palmetto. Up and up. I lose sight of him among the palm fronds. There is a bird's scream, a beating, a fluttering of wings. On and on, more bitter cries. I can't see up there. Then a long silence and the rat sneaks down from his sin. Was it eggs or babies that he ate? I hope the mother robin gets drunk.

In the succeeding days, as my energy returns, I review the years since Harriet's birth and wonder how I've come to this pass, almost as though I'd been looking for trouble.

We've had a lot of sickness: Alec has had two mastoidectomies, pneumonia, and a series of big, ugly infections from tiny scratches; oh, how many steaming flaxseed poultices I applied. I've had a tonsillectomy, an appendectomy, and a threatened hysterectomy. I had mentioned to Dr. Robey that sometimes my periods were a little heavy and that I had to go to the bathroom once in the night. Right off I was in the hands of the "best" gynecologist, Dr. B. Dr. B said that I must have a hysterectomy. "The time's coming," he said, "The time's coming when every woman will routinely have her uterus removed by the age of thirty-five." He scared me. He was a surgeon without compassion. I asked Dr. Huntington to attend the operation to save everything possible. To me a hysterectomy, if not necessary, is a mutilation of body integrity. It turned out there was nothing basically wrong — "the uterus slightly tipped." Then Dr. B tied off my fallopian tubes without permission, an invitation to promiscuity if I so wished; he palpated my gallbladder and felt stones there; then he rectified a cystocele ("took a tuck" in the bladder, I was told — was it so bad after four children to get up once in the night?). Was this a retaliatory gesture? Suddenly he succeeded. He sewed me up so tightly there it caused me permanent discomfort. And before I left the hospital I had my first gallbladder attack.

When the time came to take the stitches out of the very long belly scar, Dr. B asked if I'd like to do it myself. I couldn't bear to have him even touch me again so I took the forceps and the scissors and one by one neatly pulled out the dark stitches. He and the nurse watched surprised. "I always ask my patients as a joke. You're the first one to take me up on it."

One of these operations was fun. Jock, age four, and I were spending the night at the Robeys' in town, he to have a tonsillectomy the next morning at the Children's Hospital. I woke about midnight to feel a pain in my abdomen ripping at me. It grew steadily more intense, then almost intolerable. At seven I woke Dr. Robey, who at once called his surgeon friend, Dr. Y. Dr. Y would have his son, with whom he often operated, come to the house at once. He arrived. "Clearly appendicitis," he said. "My father and I will operate."

Young Dr. Y was so nice and friendly I asked if they could do the job under local anesthesia. He looked puzzled and surprised.

"Why?" he asked.

"Because ether gives me the horrors that last for days, and I've always wanted to watch an operation. Please, if you can."

"You'll be uncomfortable."

"I don't mind. Better than ether."

Vivid in my memory was that hell during and after childbirth. Equally vivid, if more remote, was my dissecting of animals in biology courses at college, my keeping of that well-loved dissecting kit as a possession which stood for a road not taken —

54

the medical career I was too dumb to pursue. Now I could see our three young sons bending over a plank on which I had stretched out a dead animal, could see my hands dissecting cleanly to explain to the boys the similarities of their anatomy with the animal's. They were fascinated. Three beloved towheads bent down to see more vividly.

The animals could be anything — a run-over cat, a woodchuck, squirrel, duck, rabbit. And once a mouse, neck broken in a cheese-baited snap trap. This was a treasure. Inside the placenta were three pale pink pea-sized babies. As I explained I felt as if I crooned my words. But I had never seen a real operation.

Dr. Y, Jr., responded to my eagerness.

"You'll have to watch by looking up at the reflecting mirrors on the ceiling." That was okay. My last words to Padre were, "Cancel Jock's tonsillectomy. I've got to be with him in the hospital."

Soon I lay on the operating table, a screen between me and my scrubbed abdomen. But looking up through the bright lights, I could see. I could see!

Shot after swift shot of novocaine. Then the incision, unfelt, then my guts drawn out to lie reddish and convoluted on the sterile cloth.

Once I made some casual remark about the work those four rubber gloves were doing. Dr. Y, Sr., remarked sharply, "Can that woman see what we're doing?"

"Yes," I told him. "In the overhead mirrors." He grunted and went on. So his son hadn't told him.

The badly swollen appendix was cut off, the bit of intestine stitched up, and then the rest of the mass was thrust back any old way, it seemed, through the small abdominal slit. And that *was* pain, a curious deep, dull rebellion. I forced my body to stay relaxed. The sewing up was swift and now I lay limp, tired but happy.

I had no nausea, no gas pains, and was allowed home on the third post-op day, instead of the tenth, unheard of then. I never told anyone what I had seen — not even Alec — for I was ashamed at being so crazy.

And now, as I recline on the porch, my depression lifting, listening to the rustle and rattle of the dead palmetto fronds, I wonder why I do such things. Must I feel guilty? Yes. Like Mrs. Robey, "It isn't done." Yet I do them because I want to. I need to. Yes, crazy, fun, macabre, and soul-satisfying. I had dared. The Devil was attractive.

Didn't so much physical sickness mean a more pervasive spiritual sickness as well?

Depression. Whoop it up. Bootleg or homemade liquor, like bathtub gin, flowing strong. On the seacoast, rumrunners something to watch for. Rotgut bad medicine, that homemade liquor. At one large cocktail party everyone brought their own brand of alcohol and poured it over a cake of ice set in a huge punchbowl. A lot got drunk. Alec got drunk. He also got hives. Drink some more. Make love, copulate with someone, preferably in a backyard or a field of long grass. I was lucky. My brain split with pain after two drinks. The music goes round and round. Experiments tried; couples exchange mates.

One night, off on a two-couple weekend somewhere, we made one try and one only. Next morning Alec and I giggled over the fact that "she" was totally frigid — I had learned to contract my vagina rhythmically. "He" had premature ejaculation. But still they were a merry couple and fun to drink with. Love affairs. Short-lived. Guilt too great. But oh, the joy of having a man openly admire you just because you are special and original and not just a dogsbody.

Was Alec's affair ever consummated? I never asked. So naive a man was he, he talked too much about Kathy. He had me worrying about her health as much as he, so I asked her to the beach cottage for a week, kept her mostly in bed, fire going, fed her delicious meals, gave her all my caring on a platter, babied, coddled, and listened to her rather pathetic life story and all about her husband's sadism. (I believed her. I saw it once at a dinner party.) By the time we went home, she adored me. She hadn't needed a lover, but a mother. She never plagued Alec with calls again.

The post-Prohibition cocktail lounge on the second floor of the Ritz was always busy, couples half hidden by high-backed armchairs. Alec and I spotted each other once and winked. I couldn't see who he was with. This was a Depression game— play at sexuality. One no longer felt a natural fury at betrayal, but there was guilt all right with me. I was playing with fire.

Depression. Pinch, scrape, make do, invent, go without. Uncle Tom came from Rhode Island weekly, dug me a garden, and showed me every step of nature's productivity. The lessons included wiping my tools with an oily rag when I was through. I packed away dozens of eggs in crocks of waterglass in a cool, dark basement. Dozens of chickens were boiled, soup condensed, the meat sterilized in glass jars, the skin cut in strips and fried into cracklings for cocktails; tomatoes and vegetables jarred as our forebears did. (But I would never again be a friend to Spam or fatty hamburg.)

The boys and I stood in the five-and-ten. "Please, please, it's only ten cents." Brother, can you spare a dime? I knew that my refusal meant I was making them scapegoats for some of my own personal indulgences. After all, there was money for cigarettes and alcohol.

Yes, we have no bananas, we have no bananas today. Dancing, parties, drinking, worry, businesses failing, making merry. One day while folding diapers in the basement I knew I simply could not face the dinner dance at the Andover Country Club that night. We were part of a table for twelve. I knew no one. New people still scared me silent. Then a stroke of genius. If I looked at each man as if I adored him, maybe someone would dance

57

with me. I practiced a bit in front of the mirror. Sitting at the long table among all the others, I looked across at the man opposite me and smiled my adoring, worshiping smile, my eyes darting out love signals. He looked at me. "Let's dance," he said. Back at the table I did the same with the left- and right-hand men. The same thing happened. Before the evening was over I was the focus of the stag line. Some of us took the soft-centered round buns off the butter plates and tried to hit the wall telephone at the other end of the big room. I was drunk only with a wonderful sense of freedom, of power and joyousness that people could like me.

The next morning at Mother's in Tewksbury she asked how the dance was. I said, "Lots of fun." She looked at me suspiciously. Christ, she could always read my mind.

"Are you living up to your standards?" Her face was deeply concerned. She always has known, she always will know. I went home utterly deflated after my one delicious fling.

Our eight-year-old son, when asked what he especially wanted for his birthday, said, "That you and Daddy never go out for cocktails again." Staggered, I had to feel around that one. I reviewed the whole scene, of Alec coming back and either taking the baby-sitter home or hurrying the children to bed and out of his sight, I tucking them in overlovingly, oversolicitously, in imitation of my usual goodnight hug. Children know the difference, all right. So I told him it was a grown-up world, that is what people did nowadays, but we would go out less. And when we did go, we would come back "ourselves." No more oversweet imitation.

The Depression. Alec had his mill job and hated it. It was no field for him. It took imagination, foresight, and quick decisions, but the "family" didn't feel they could fire him. I guessed it all. I worked on committees, on charities, with the Red Cross — a good Depression matron, eating up what little energy there was. I was on the edge of cracking and running to Florida and Mother.

With the two little ones in tow, I took the train north and home to find that Sandy has gone depressed too. (The appendectomy at that particular age? My absence? Or his father?) He sits most of the time playing idly and listlessly with little Harriet's toys. I can do for a child what I couldn't do for myself — make an appointment with a recommended analyst, Dr. John Murray. His office is as unthreatening as he is. We discuss Sandy, and Beata Rank, the only child analyst, is contacted. At the end I timidly say that I have no energy and feel I am a spoiled child. I should dismiss any household help and do a decent day's work — drive myself. Master inertia. Get so tired I'll sleep. Doesn't that make sense?

It doesn't. I'm soon in that alien and fearful world of a Freudian psychoanalysis, driving daily to Boston, lying on a dark maroon couch with *Him* behind me relaxed on armchair and footstool. My extended family has always been scornful of any weakness. Psychoanalysis means sick, sick, sick. Psychiatrists are out to get you by having you come to the office every day for years. And the money is coming from Mother.

CHAPTER 9

Learning Family through Psychoanalysis

ACH DAY, I climb the brownstone steps and inspect the six well-shined nameplates, just in case Dr. Murray's office has magically disappeared. Then I enter the huge hall, nod to the two secretaries at their desks beside the front door, and climb the wide, three-angled stairs. This must have been a very luxurious town house once. Now it is as silent as a tomb with all humankind closed either in or out.

I enter "my" waiting room, opening and shutting the door softly. I'm always early as if by being late something awful will happen: that *he* will go away or tell me *he* never wants to see me again. There is an empty fireplace in the room, a sofa, and three armchairs, one with a lamp and magazine table beside it. It is on this chair I always sit and wait, wait and listen. Once I heard howling sobs coming faintly down the flue, reverberation making the sound unearthly — a woman patient on the third floor above me? I hear the double soundproof door of his room to the hall open, open — close, close.

I hold my breath. What's waiting for me today? Now the click of the doorknob. Now the sound of him taking a few steps along the short passage. My door opens up. His mild face and smile greet me impersonally. I go into his office, closing doors behind me. I lie down in my accustomed posture as he settles himself out of sight behind me.

On the very first visit I sat in an armchair opposite him while he explained in detail the theory and regimen of analysis and the reasons for it. Now, well-acquainted with the routine and seeing nothing but ceiling if I open my eyes, I can forget my self-consciousness in his presence, except when he speaks, which is seldom. I slip into the dreamlike flow of free associations. Here on this maroon couch I learn to be daring, to speak freely of shameful things, to curse freely — to be cleanly and freely angry. I learn that anger can be directed straight at Dr. Murray. I learn to flow freely until the lost again is found, and that becomes an extraordinarily enjoyable experience. For every word that comes out of my mouth unbidden is another moment of astonishment. Now I know that the "I" I thought I was is not the "I" that I am. The last vestiges of the precious and guarded little princess disappear like mist, as slowly, month by month, I become tougher, wiser, more suspicious, yet at the same time more compassionate.

I can finally view Mrs. Robey with real pity. The discovery amazes me. And Dr. Murray amazes me. He is so humane, friendly, and wise, so unthreatening, so orderly, and, occasionally, so cross with me. I begin building many fantasies around Dr. Murray. Too many.

Within a week of the first session I feel dance in my steps and dance in my mind. Now I am alive and totally sensate again; yet I also feel premonitions of some new awfulness awaiting me. I swing wildly between joy and terror. The terror, however, is only anticipation of the unknown.

As I begin to understand my hidden and my primitive impulses, I translate that understanding into universal human behavior. Mentally I analyze all the actions of our families that I can't understand. That's dangerous. I talk too much in glowing excitement. How strange life is! Until now, I never realized our feelings, our personalities, our drives came from anywhere except instinct.

It is a while before I learn to keep my mouth shut about my analysis, but by then I have become a "non-person" among relatives and old friends. "Get out of it," they urge me. "Quick. That quack has you caught; he's just after your money and he's changing your lovely, gentle personality." I learn to dismiss them.

Part of me works to recreate myself. Another — unknown — part of me appears in memories which come as if from nowhere, one by one, all in due time.

I understand more clearly my sense of guilt and original sin. Specifically, I recall attacking my baby brother, who had just been born. Murder in my three-year-old heart. I know I didn't hurt him much. I wasn't strong enough. But to hate is to kill. So I had murdered.

I recall playing with myself in my crib. My fingers still remember the touch that had been so pleasurable. Suddenly Mother stood above me once and hissed, "Never!" Her face was as deadly as that of one of the Furies.

I had committed a terrible sin. I had told a lie. Waking in a nightmare, I went out into the hall. From below there came the lovely smell of Father's pipe and the friendly light from his little study. I cried hard. Mother came fast. I told her I had a leg ache, a headache, a stomachache, a backache — but I knew I didn't have any of these. Or did I? If I didn't, why was my eardrum punctured daily in the doctor's office for a week? The first time he opened the drum the pain was so terrible I screamed. Then it became intensely pleasurable.

I recall the year we moved to Tewksbury to a very old house on an isolated road. I had a nightly dream. On the double railroad tracks in the valley below the hill was a crossing guarded by a man who came out of his little house and waved his red flag. Father regularly warned us to stop, look to right and left, to listen. In the dream I jumped from one track to the other, but no matter which track I chose a train bore down on me.

The cowcatcher caught me up, ground me to bits, and spewed me out. I loved that sense of being violently and painfully destroyed.

And analysis is my first chance to tell myself and somebody else about Uncle Tom and how difficult that old witch Mrs. Robey is.

"A witch?" Dr. Murray asks. "How so?"

"Well, she's a witch to me."

"She's a neurotic woman."

"Am I neurotic?"

"Yes."

I begin to cry. Another time Dr. Murray uses the word "hate." I protest, saying I've never hated anyone in my life.

"No?" A long silence. Again I cry.

At last I am able to talk about Uncle Tom. It is a long time in coming, but it comes.

The memory comes out painfully and slowly, yet with such stark immediacy. As it opens up, guilt floods me.

I adored Uncle Tom. I felt so sorry for him, as did Mother and Father. The woman he had loved for years and wanted to marry had just chosen another man and Uncle Tom began to feed me the love I felt I didn't get from Father. Father was so repressed in all his emotions and it seemed to me that he preferred my sister, who was lively and could make him laugh. I was twelve when Uncle Tom taught me to drive his Packard on the empty country roads, I sitting on a cushion and looking through the steering wheel. He drove me to school. I worked in his garden with him and learned to be precise and careful in my motions. He brought me wonderful things. Without anyone to play with, I followed him like a shadow. He was my Daddy-Long-Legs (from a favorite book of mine, all about an older man loving a little girl). At least once a week I went to his house for supper and Mother encouraged this, for at his house I ate well — crisp broiled chops, baked potato, a vegetable salad, and some fine dessert cooked by his tiny grizzled maid, Fanny. At home I disliked food, ate little, and was very thin. Later, I learned to call my condition anorexia.

Gradually the regular pattern emerged. After supper we crossed the hall to the living room and he drew the heavy portiere across the entrance. Then he pulled all the shades exactly to the sill, put another log on the fire, went to his mahogany humidor, and took out a fine Havana cigar. With his very clean, white hands — red hairs on the back — the nails close-cut and with ridges on them, he took from his pocket his cigar cutter and nipped a small and accurate V on one end of the cigar, then rolled it over his lips to wet it before he lit the other end. The smell of the smoke was delicious. Then he opened up the card table, pulled down the legs one by one, and set it by the sofa while I got out the cards precisely from their case. Then I played Solitaire and he watched. He paid me ten cents for every card I built up into suits. Sometimes he would giggle. After several games he put away the card table with the same exactness and turned out the lights because firelight was enough and we sat side by side on the sofa again. First his hand patted my knee, then stroked it, then slid up my panties. And he touched and rubbed that area that should never be touched even by myself. I sat tense, waiting for it to be over but I must do as Uncle Tom wished.

When he finally said it was time for me to go home and to bed, I got up quickly. Sometimes he walked across the road with me, but he always stopped to wash his hands first. That, to me, was the most horrible shame. Other times, if I went home alone, I flew out his driveway, across the road, and into my own driveway as if devils were after me.

And always Mother welcomed me back and said, so pleasantly, "What did you and Uncle Tom do tonight?"

Once I stayed with him while Mother and Father were in Florida. When I was ready for bed, he tucked me in as if I were a very little girl. He kissed me goodnight gently, opened the window, turned out the lights, and went out, closing the door. But one night, instead of leaving, he stood there close by the bed in the dark, silent, silent. Why didn't he go! Why won't he go! In the dark he made no motion whatever. Go. Go. I sensed an awful tension in that stillness. I lay motionless. Go. Go. I breathed deeply as if I were asleep. What was he standing right there for? His tension was mine now. At long last I heard him move noiselessly out of the room. The door closed softly. I almost sobbed in my relief. I did not think, and I did not know. But I was part of something I did not understand. Poor Uncle Tom.

Dr. Murray assures me that such things are not uncommon and did me no harm except for the guilt. I tell him I didn't know then what a kept woman was, but that I had all the feelings of one — paid for my services — and that my shame lay like lead within me. I say that I both loved and hated him.

"How long did it go on?"

I don't know. I do remember when I got my first period, quite late, that I asked Mother to tell Father to tell Uncle Tom. But he still gave me things. He insisted that I wasn't strong enough to go to college, but I was determined and I did. And in my first two months there I gained twenty pounds. Away from home at last.

Still I cannot deal with my feelings about Mother. No way can I be angry with her. I have taken too much and not given enough and she is paying for all these analytic hours. Month after month I slide and slip away from seeing her as anything but purity and love. I *will not* look. But in that peaceful room, as I see deeper and deeper into those places in my mind that have no known location yet finally fuse into a specific memory or emotion, there comes a dream which I pour out to Dr. Murray. Mother and I are on a Cunard liner, shipwrecked off the tip of the point at the beach. We are alone; everyone else

65

has drowned. I am trying desperately to escape death. I turn to Mother for help, but find her face one of vicious Medusa rage. Every move I make, cabin to cabin, companionway to stairs, trying to get out and up into the air, Mother is after me — a furious and insane female blocking my way or pulling me back.

At last I elude her in my own death panic, and she, beyond reason, suddenly appears before me holding a poison bomb and flings it into my face. It is the final betrayal. And just as I die, I wake shaken, but furious at the woman whom I had always believed honestly loved me.

Now I can begin to follow the complicated emotions that can flow unknown from mother to daughter . . .

The first months of analysis are very bad for Alec. This period is so private and beautiful that I don't want to share details. But Alec senses a change in me and becomes very aggressive, cold, and ugly to me and the children. He drinks more heavily. He is utterly impossible. One stormy analytic hour I jerk off my wedding ring and throw it across the room.

"Go pick it up and put it on," Dr. Murray says sternly. I cower inside, obey, groveling under his desk to retrieve that band of servitude. He doesn't move. I then cry out against the strictures of Alex's and my incompatibility. Another fateful day in Dr. Murray's office, I announce that Alec will have to have analysis himself or I can't take it any longer. (I say I'll even get a divorce, knowing how idle is that threat. There are no divorces in our extensive family. You're supposed to grin and bear anything.) Dr. Murray tells me Alec can't be analyzed. Violent and primitive emotions are too near the surface and, paradoxically, too deep. No, Alec would probably go to pieces if he were to open up his feelings. If I do stay with him I'll have to do all the work myself.

That is the death knell to my hopes.

Or is it a challenge?

Alec tells me one day that he's been in to see Dr. Murray. I gape. All by his big, little timid self. "Dig your fingers into your palms, but wait," Alec quoted Dr. Murray as saying. So it's up to me, as usual.

I begin sharing with Alec all I dare — nothing about himself and almost nothing about his mother, but a lot about the feelings I couldn't bring out about my mother and some of the things she did. I give in detail my many newfound childhood memories. We discover we can laugh ruefully at them. Each night I communicate what I feel he can tolerate and, *mirabile dictu*, he sporadically spurts out some of his own.

Alec's earliest recall was when Nana would bring him, a toddler, to his mother as she lay in bed in the morning. And Mrs. Robey would bounce him and hold him at arm's length above her and pull him down against her body and hold him up again, laughing. A wonderful game! I could imagine Alec crowing with delight. But when Mrs. Robey saw or realized he had an erection, she hit him hard and sent him back to Nana. However, the game must have had its peculiar fascination for both because it was many times repeated.

Another memory: Alec was little and playing with toys on the floor. Mrs. Robey and Puss Leaman were sitting on the sofa near him. Puss Leaman was looking at her with a funny look, saying very softly, "Will you? Do you? Tell me you do!" And Mrs. Robey said nothing but looked at Mr. Leaman. Alec wanted to kill him.

Another memory: Alec was about six or seven years old and getting ten cents allowance a week, five to go into the plate at church — he attended the full, long Congregational sermon — and five cents for himself, which he invariably spent on a small brown bag of unshelled peanuts. He adored peanuts. One day Mrs. Robey discovered two bags in his coat pocket and forced out of him the fact that he had only pretended to put the five cents in the plate. Though it was a scant two or three days before Christmas, Mrs. Robey returned all the presents she or her friends planned to give Alec, with the statement that this was a day of disgrace. She let the maids take a three-day holiday and put the Christmas decorations out of sight.

Dr. and Mrs. Robey and Alec spent Christmas in a small country inn. Mrs. Robey never spoke once to Alec. All day she sat and stared or glared at him. (Much as her father, Mr. Alexander, must have done with her — hence her childhood cry, "Poppa eye me.") So now I could understand why Alec so hated Christmas and anything to do with it.

And yet another memory: when Alec was sixteen his mother took him on a grand tour of Europe. They were staying at a hotel high in the Alps and two American girls about Alec's age were there with their parents. One day he and the girls climbed a mountain above the village. (Even then Alec was pretty brash with his strength, I imagine, for at the beach club in the summer he loved to grab other teenagers and throw them into the water. Eventually he was ordered to stop.) There, high up on that Swiss mountain, were some great single boulders. He found one that was not too solidly set. With all his might he was able to rock it a bit and then start it, off balance, rolling down the mountainside. Great was the amusement of the three as it bounced, leaped high, and crash-dash tumbled faster and faster out of sight.

When they got down to the village again, there was a mob of people standing around. A rock had fallen down the mountain and killed a man. Alec looked. It was his rock!

I couldn't believe it. "Why in God's name didn't you tell me about this before? And what happened next?" I demanded.

"I've never thought of it since," Alec said. "I don't remember what happened next because I got sick with something and we had to change our itinerary."

During my first winter of analysis a young writer who was going abroad for the season asked Mrs. Robey if she would like his pedigreed English fox terrier while he was away. She was delighted. She had had a fox terrier for Alec when he was a little boy, and we had them for our own children. The first night, the high-strung dog, shut up in the bathroom, howled inconsolably. Mrs. Robey tried to quiet it, but it kept howling. Then she struck the dog. It continued howling. Mrs. Robey told me, without shame or compunction, how she beat it across the face until it cowered and went silent. Shut up again in the bathroom, the dog howled even louder until she went in and hit it over and over with all her might. Silence. The dog groveled on its belly into a corner and stayed there. Silence remained as she got into bed again.

The next day the terrier took to following her slavishly and blindly. She was pleased at first, but he would not move from her side. He had no life but her, sitting close, touching her skirts, unmoving. If she shifted her leg slightly, he would shift too. She became more and more irritated, frustrated, and enraged. Finally she couldn't bear it any longer and had the dog destroyed. Hearing Mrs. Robey talk about the terrier, I could only think of Alec in his childhood . . .

Day after day I climb those brownstone steps and glance at the brass plates, and Alec and I grow closer because we are sharing deep and long-lost secrets. I understand now why he has been cowed by his mother and yet has remained tied to her. Now I know why he must build bigger and better granite walls and terraces that will never move. Now I know why he was always cold to Puss Leaman. I also understand about other compulsions of his. And he knows a lot about my problems and he loves it when I eventually break through and express the rage I feel toward my own mother.

Dr. Murray points out that I've wasted months denying and blocking. Also that I'm very angry at myself. And I get to work, and enter a new hell of terror and depression. Is Mother reading my mind? For a couple of months she forgets to send her check. Then all is as before in the love that flows between us, though its waters are perhaps less pellucid.

Day after day, learning more and more, I climb those steps. Day after day I walk down them and back to my family. Meanwhile Alec is gaining security. With security comes nerve and defiance. Perhaps he's a fool to criticize his mother, perhaps he's wise. In any case he gives her both barrels and the inevitable result is a letter.

Dearest Cunck,

On both your trips to Stonington, you made dogmatic charges for which you undoubtedly thought you had foundation or you could not have been so cruel to any Lady. You said, "You haven't the foggiest notion about modern psychology." You stated that, "Whether you know it or not, you hated your father and mother when you were a child." I am ready to swear that any hatred or resentment that my father may have aroused at times, there was never the slightest of either where Mother was concerned, for even when very young I realized that she was not personally responsible for what seemed like an irrational severity or unwarranted punishment. I don't know that I worked that out, but children sense many things they can't rationalize about. My mother was the only person I have ever met who was the personification of love, yet strangely enough, as the years have passed, I have come to realize that it was my father who influenced me more than she and who left a deeper imprint, probably because of the intellectual stimulus he gave and the force of his really memorable character. I would give a great deal to have something of the grace and spirit which were my mother's.

You also said that I have an alcohol complex, whatever that may be. If you resent that I do not enjoy seeing anyone intoxicated, even my own son, you are absolutely right, but since I both serve and take alcohol the idea of a complex is mystifying.

You said I had given you an inferiority complex and although not familiar with that term, when you were very young you may remember that I stopped trying to teach you when my many shortcomings were borne in on me, and that I did not resume until it seemed evident that we could work harmoniously together. If that inferiority complex is in any degree responsible for the overbearing arrogance — now such a striking characteristic — I can never forgive myself.

You are so precious to me, so infinitely precious, and I am proud of all that is so fine and noble in you (and I recognize with joy a great deal). But the wounds you have inflicted may loom larger than they should; in any event, I am the mother who loves you and has always loved you.

C.S.

Now I begin to understand Isabelle Robey. I add to this that she had once mentioned the great loss of an older sister who had mothered her when she was tiny. Perhaps Mathilda Torrens Alexander had herself been depressed by the loss of four children, with the sixth one, Isabelle, born when she was forty-two. Did Isabelle perhaps try to make up for the son her father must have wanted?

The bitterness has long since gone out of my hindsight and only compassion is left. Alec and I were both battered children in a way; battered by love, possessed by love, repressed by love, love that held many archaic elements.

But that bit of selflessness and honesty in Mrs. Robey's letter was startling. How casual and careless we of the younger generation always are of the people who are our parents and who, we blindly assume, can take care of themselves.

Day after day I climb those steps, enter Dr. Murray's office, and take my accustomed place. Once, without thinking, I get up on one elbow and twist my head to look at him. He is sitting with his feet on his stool, a large bunch of seedless green grapes in his hand. He pops the grapes rhythmically one by one into his mouth.

CHAPTER 10

The Robeys' Financial Secret Is Out

UDDENLY ALEC and I catch on. When did the limousine and Brian, the chauffeur, go? When did the Robeys stop renting the big house on the hill in Connecticut and take a far smaller one in the village where Isabelle could walk to the beach club? When had that winter coat of hers become so shabby and worn? We have taken it all for granted. Now, suddenly, our family has shifted on its axis. The old patterns and reactions are no longer valid.

Now Alec is searching out his father. He and Dr. Robey had never grown close or confided in one another. Was that because Isabelle never liked to have anybody talk out of her hearing, or did Hal Robey never reach out to his son?

One day by coincidence they were alone in the house. Hal Robey's rage about Puss Leaman burst forth. Isabelle would never hear anything said against him. Yet his financial advice had been incredibly bad. Even I, in 1923, buying my wedding slippers, saw that the shoes in the store seemed very old-fashioned. Isabelle would not consider a younger manager. Moreover, Puss Leaman was buying common stock for her on margin. At some point she had made a $100,000 loan to him. The store had been dying and the stock-market crash killed everything.

Puss told her she must keep on paying the taxes on the now unused property because the Depression would not last more than a few months. Year after year during the 1930's, she shelled out what I think was $75,000 per year in city taxes for the property near the northwest corner of Fifth Avenue and Forty-Second Street. Now she was absolutely penniless. In 1934 Dr. Robey was sixty-five and had to retire from the faculty at Harvard Medical School. His days were no longer spent at Boston City Hospital. His private patients were getting old and few, so he took on insurance cases. There were no other resources or recourses. By the time the Robeys' money was gone, so was Puss Leaman's. He had been let go some years before from two brokerage houses. For dishonesty? For bad judgment?

Dr. Robey told Alec about the time at the camp at Lake Umbagog when he was standing on the pier and Puss Leaman was on the porch cleaning his guns. A shot whizzed by, almost clipping his ear. Dr. Robey yelled up to the porch, "What the hell!"

"I didn't realize the gun was loaded," Puss said, but Hal Robey was sure that he was being deliberately shot at. He knew about Isabelle's crazy $100,000 loan, which he also knew would never be paid back. Hal Robey detested Puss Leaman. He always had.

He told Alec about Isabelle's stubbornness. On their honeymoon at Bretton Woods she insisted on separate rooms. When she got back to Roxbury and his home and office, she took one look around, went out and climbed onto a horsecar, went to the Back Bay, and took the first train to New York. Her father raged. "Woman, go back to your wedded husband. God has told you to serve, to cleave, to obey." By this time Hal had caught up with her and added his pleas. She returned to Boston with reluctance and in fear of her father. From then

73

on Hal, too, was like the dog that had been whipped. All those years of Puss Leaman's presence in the house, the patience with which Hal hid his hate — the passivity he had to develop.

Things were very, very bad in the House of Robey. Yet not so bad in some ways. She was becoming gentler, more thoughtful of Hal, and far too admiring of me.

Christmas Day, 1940, arrived. We drove to Commonwealth Avenue. It was mild and sunny. We had the top of the car down. The children loved these recently initiated Christmases. In the center of the dining-room table was a great round tin dough pan covered with red crepe paper. From the sides, leading out to each seat, were red ribbons ending with the children's names on scraps of white cards. Hal carved the turkey at the long serving table before the south windows. The children wiggled and eyed the Christmas "pie." When Isabelle said, "Now!" each pulled on a ribbon that ended with a little present. Oh, she had been ingenious. She was giving away all the little unnecessary things in the house — family accumulations, a photo, a pen, a wallet; things from Hal's office — rubber bands, a ruler, a candy bar — and on and on. I watched the joy in her smile. I saw Hal's benign face, and Alex's relaxation. And for dessert, there were "alligators" — the great treat made by Katy, meringues in the rough shape of alligators, with long curving tails, open jaws, and *big red eyes* of half cherries.

This year we have a surprise. Back up in the living room, the children and Alex disappear momentarily. The three boys return carrying a large carton with a huge red bow on top. They place it before Isabelle, who is standing at the fireplace. She pulls off the bow and up pops "Miss Robey," holding a furrier's box. She opens it, sees the black caracul-paw coat (the best we dare buy), turns, puts her head down on the mantel, and heaves with dreadful silent sobs. We are all aghast. When she has mastered this incredible emotion, gaiety begins.

Harriet is never again called "Miss Robey." Now that the

Robey poverty is out in the open (albeit only partially), now that Isabelle can tell me with pride of the eighteen-dollar dress she got at a sale, or how Katy and Margaret are calcimining the very high-ceilinged rooms one by one, we suggest an apartment with Hal sharing an office with another doctor. Then one maid would do. Although she insists, "It isn't done," her protest is fainter than of yore. But the big house is too important to her, and the struggle to keep up appearances continues. And so they go on with never a complaint. Now and then a couple for bridge — a nice little dinner served.

I finally understand someone whom I occasionally see coming or going, a scuttling little man who has borne away jewelry, silver, crystal, and china. Since she never refers to him or his work, I assume this is her greatest shame.

The Pietà comes strongly to my mind. Here are mother and son in an exquisite representation of humankind's most tragic and beautiful myth — death, resurrection, and transfiguration. In the statue, Mary is so pure, so immaculate, so innocent sexually: she looks about eighteen years old instead of fifty. Christ himself appears to be a late adolescent as, freed from his agony of the cross and the pain of life, he is the universal dead son wiped out by the darker passions of man. I visualize the soft joy in Mary's face and see the whole myth of mother and son brought to a beauty that is unearthly. Why else is the greatest taboo incest between mother and son?

Poor Isabelle, poor mothers.

CHAPTER 11

The Social-Work Student

THE IMPLICATIONS of the Pietà, as yet not fully understood by me but giving me strange longings, turn my thoughts to parental responsibilities. Where do we suffer and where do we sacrifice for the next generation?

Dr. Lewis Perry at Phillips Exeter Academy had earlier told us the boys would lose not one, but probably two, years in grade unless they went to private schools. It is on his advice that we send the two older ones to the Fenn School in Concord.

The time has come for me to dictate. I decide that we must move to Cambridge to put all four children into the progressive Shady Hill School. I am thankful that Alec makes no audible protest, but he is very unhappy when we move. I rent furnished, at $125 a month, a four-square house with about ten feet of land on all sides. Dull but adequate. I apply for graduate school at Radcliffe — English — to learn to write. I have to fight the formidable Dean Beatrice Cronkhite for acceptance. My grades sixteen years before were too poor.

Leaving our beloved stone stable is very hard on everyone. Alec will lose his workshop, his creations, his partying and acting friends. He will be in a house where he cannot make alterations. Mother, poor Mother, is losing the treasure of a stable she had created for us so generously, but which has put me in such terrible unacknowledged debt. I will be leaving all my furniture in the house and take responsibility for renting the castle apartments and the stable itself. She will get the same income as she did before. And that's the best I can do. We reassemble, pick up old friends, and Alec begins acting with three new groups.

These are pleasant and gay years. Then Pearl Harbor strikes everybody's lives. The two older boys go into the navy. Dr. Murray is called to Washington, meaning the end of my analysis. Too soon. I have hardly killed Mother.

We're expanding emotionally. We're probably in Cambridge permanently, and we buy a house near Harvard Square that is a replica of a large old Salem mansion. The house once belonged to Professor L. J. Henderson. Its fame rested on the fact that Dr. Henderson kept the temperature at about 50 degrees and those entertained by him wore overcoats, even at the dinner table; and on the other fact that Harvard's President Eliot broke his arm going down the front steps. It is a fine house for us. The first thing we do is put on storm windows and install a new furnace.

At the beginning of the war Alec is sent by the mill to Australia to evaluate the availability of their particularly fine merino wool. We need a cable address since he will be gone for over three months. He comes up with "Kitten, Cambridge." Kitten is his pet loving name for me. He had started with "Happy," my college nickname, then "Hap," then "Happit." And then he turns up with "Kitten" from a colored Christmas calendar advertisement for the Chesapeake and Ohio Railroad showing "Chessie," the kitten in a bunk. It is a very cuddly kitten. After that, "Kitten" I remain.

Several times he has to cable his plans, and it is fun to hear the telephone operator ask quite coyly, "Is this 'Kitten, Cambridge'?" And I, as coyly, "Yes, this is 'Kitten, Cambridge.'"

Alec and I become block wardens and putter-outers of incendiary bombs. We know what's in everybody's attics. (Some of the Brattle Street attics are very fine, full of rejectables.) And we give orders. We have taken courses up to and including Advanced Red Cross Training. In the appeal by the government for more housing, we turn the whole top floor — six rooms and a bath — into a rentable apartment.

We give the two younger children war jobs. One pulls down all the blackout shades at dusk and rolls them up in the morning, the other is out on the streets to report any crack of window light in our district.

I work as a volunteer part-time at the Harvard Psychological Clinic under Dr. Harry Murray (no relation of my own Dr. Murray). I can't bear it, fascinating as it is. Young college lads are paid seventy-five cents an hour to go through all the tests, including electric shocks, and to have their personalities stripped down to the last dark place. They are then let go. And there is no psychiatric help at Harvard's Stillman Infirmary or the Health Clinic.

I boldly make an appointment with the great Dr. Helene Deutsch, who knows more about women than anyone else. I tell her that since Dr. Murray left, I've been depressed, I need to work and want to become a doctor.

"What for?"

"To be a psychiatrist and help others."

"A waste. You'll have to forget most of what you learn. Social work is gaining eminence fast. I myself am teaching students in the field. Eventually your training will be such that you'll be doing the treatment you want."

Sitting in Dean Hardwick's office at the Simmons School of Social Work, I plead for a chance to enroll. Again, as at Radcliffe, I have to fight for growth. There is great gravity about Dean Hardwick — a tall, white-haired, dignified lady social worker, her specialty being community organization. "Too old, much too old. Forty-three? No one over thirty has ever graduated. All who tried failed or could not manage families and the responsibilities of their career."

I explain about analysis. This seems to make her taller and more righteous. "Yes, we have psychiatric courses here under Mrs. Solomon — and Mrs. Bandler teaches casework. But you're too old. We cannot accept you." She rises, goes to the door, opens it, stands there, righteous and disapproving. I leave.

I go straight to the Boston University School of Social Work, have a good interview, and am accepted. But I still want Simmons. The next day I'm back in Miss Hardwick's office, my acceptance from Boston University in my pocket.

I plead again. I tell Miss Hardwick, "By the time a woman is no longer essential to her family, she has a great storehouse of love, caring, self-control, self-determination, and patience." I tell her my mind is uncluttered. "I think you should at least give me a try," I add. And I stand there.

The grudging reply: "All right. But on trial. You've had too much fancy psychiatry stuff already. I'll make your field placement tough — in Public Assistance. Then you'll see what social work really is. The new semester starts next Monday. Report to me." So she has a good social worker's heart after all.

Alec is cooperative. But he never yet has said no to something I wanted very much. He will leave the house in the morning before I do and we will get back about the same time.

On the day I start at Simmons, I remove my gold Lyman seal ring. I do not want to wear it ever again. Why? I've taken the step from being a lady needing props to a woman. The ring can wait for my daughter's eighteenth birthday, just as Father gave me and my sister ours at that age. The thought comes to mind that I'm a biological sport out of my environment.

The work is three days in the classroom taking courses or studying and two days in the field within an assigned agency. It turns out that I am to be, not in Public Assistance, but in AFDC (Aid to Families with Dependent Children). I enter a great room filled with social workers sitting at their rows of desks and files. Miss Mahoney, an ex-schoolteacher with a nice sense of humor, is my supervisor and responsible for all I learn and do in practical work. The district I am to serve in is the worst in Boston.

She gives me my first case along with the agency guidelines. "Always wear a hat. Never sit in an overstuffed chair — you'll get bedbugs. Never accept tea or coffee. If you're alone with a child, ask him if 'Daddy' has been around. Pull open closet doors to see if any man's pants are hanging there. Be cool and businesslike."

I enjoy my visit. I don't wear a hat, I sit at the kitchen table to drink the offered coffee, and a neat little woman and I have a good chat. Slum housing, but a very clean Salvation Army–supplied flat.

I do a detailed handwritten report on the condition of the place and family and give it to Miss Mahoney on my next day there. She says my write-up is badly done — I didn't cross my *t*'s, dot my *i*'s, or put commas in the right places. Joy enters my soul.

"Mrs. O'Brien has cases for you. She's been overworked and she can now have some relief."

Mrs. O'Brien is a most dignified straight-backed female with a mass of white hair piled high on the very top of her head. She has on her desk a stack of twenty-eight cases. She hands them to me. "Watch this one," she says, touching the top of the pile. "It's a bad place. Each floor has people who could make trouble. There is a pervert on the first floor, a suspected murderer on the second, a schizophrenic on the third. Your client is on the fourth, an alcoholic who can be violent. Tell her if she doesn't stop drinking, we'll withdraw her allowance for the kids. Maybe she'll listen to you."

This is my challenge. I go right to it. From the outside, the dirty, yellow-brick row house looks utterly dismal. Boards are over the broken windows at each hallway level. I open the door and walk into pitch-darkness. The smell of urine and vomit is powerful. I feel for the light switch, flick it, but no light comes on. All bulbs have apparently been broken or removed. Cautiously feeling my way around the stairwell, my right hand guided by the greasy-to-the-touch wall, I begin my ascent. At last the top, light slitting through the door cracks. My foot trips over liquor bottles. So she is drinking up the AFDC allotment. A disorderly woman with uncombed hair answers my knock. She looks angry and suspicious, but I smile at her and ask her if she can tell me about the children. Grudgingly, and very guardedly, she offers coffee. I acept it with gratitude, sit in an overstuffed armchair, and watch with interest as a big bedbug moves out of the fabric and up and over my arm.

Before I'm through we're laughing and on teasing terms. I grin at her. "You're a naughty one with all those bottles." She is able to tell me some of what hurts her. I feel my way down to the street, realizing that I am able to be warm and comfortable and that I may be a good social worker after all.

Am I having too good a time? I am moved to the Family Service Association at Upham's Corner, with a Rankian-trained supervisor who is a good teacher. To get the year's credit in eight months, I have to take two summer courses at Boston University and two at Boston College. I am swallowing great gulps of knowledge. And well-advised criticism.

I'm at our beach compound in early September on one week's vacation before I start my last year in psychiatric social work. I feel hemmed in by my questioning, dubious, extended family. I have already been told that I have the plum of second-year placements, Judge Baker Child Guidance Clinic. I am to start on Tuesday, the day after Labor Day. Can I throw away all my old family attitudes toward working women? Could I truly become a social worker? On Saturday I run a temperature — I hadn't had one since 1937. On Monday night it is higher but with no symptoms. A burning 103 degrees. The analyst Beata Rank visits me in bed. "I don't care how you feel or how high your temperature is tomorrow morning. You get up, get dressed, and go to your first class."

Another choice, another deep-life change. I do as I am told, denying the clinical thermometer and its implications. My temperature is normal by the end of the day.

I think of my gold seal ring and laugh.

CHAPTER 12

Father—The First Death

I SNUGGLE UP with Alec one Monday night early in May 1949, very tired after a long weekend at the American Psychiatric Association meeting in Montreal — my first national conference. I'm almost asleep. Alec says, "Oh, I forgot. Your father had a stroke sometime last Friday night. Your mother was in bed with him and never woke." A howl rises in me. Shock and fury.

"You could have called me in Canada! I'd have come right back."

"There's nothing you could have done for him. His brain's completely destroyed. He can't move. They've got the nurses and the hospital bed in the old playroom. He's being tube-fed. Besides, the rest of your family was there."

Sleep is impossible now. But anger quiets to the aching emptiness of loss.

I find Mother quite frozen. "Oh, my darling girl! Where were you?" She cries in my arms briefly, then gains control.

The weeks pass. I spend as much time in Tewksbury as I can and I see Mother going ghostlike into Father's room, looking at the motionless mass under the sheet, slipping out again. When I'm there I do the same. She and I often talk, but not about Father. Not yet.

Now there is an embolism in his leg and the doctor and the family decide against amputation. He is kept on morphine. My sister has come to stay as long as . . . My brothers stop on their way to and from work. Father has been the wise old man of our tribe. He is eighty-five and to my knowledge he has never been ill with anything, not even a cold. He has all his teeth. How I wish I could sit motionless as he did — a philosopher or dreamer looking up and out, pipe in hand. Sometimes the smoke encircled his bald head like a wreath.

It's June 23. I can't sleep. I don't want to sleep. I slip downstairs in bare feet and nightgown. It's midsummer and very warm. I stand in the doorway a moment; this is the room once all gold, glitter, and shine with light reflecting from my many wedding presents.

Through the hours the nurse and I wait, one on each side of the bed. He has always loved the songs of Gilbert and Sullivan, and I sing or chant his favorites. This is for my own grieving, not for his comfort, but it is yet a communication of sorts. I wonder aloud if he could have an extra shot of morphine. . . .

His breathing gets worse. No inhalation for endless seconds, then great indrawing gasps. Then the awful silence again. Will he, can he breathe once more? He will, he can. But as the night passes the gasping is rougher and harder and more desperate. There is something dreadful and fascinating watching the dying body try to obey its demand for air. I hold my own breath each time — the nurse seems to also — the silence so long. Yes, it begins again — terrible, so terrible to me, yet unfelt and unknown by him.

And this time the silence is even longer. I grip the sheet — second after second after second. But there is nothing more.

"He's gone," the nurse says. I kiss his forehead.

Now I see that day has come into the room. I walk out the door to the porch and onto the dew-soaked grass where my bare feet make black patches. There is a radiance about me.

The sun, just over the horizon, makes every dewdrop sparkle like a star. I am in some incredible glory and utterly happy. Why am I allowed that beauty and what does it mean? Now, at last, I can have him. I'm in that resurrection too.

I shall never forget this moment when Father and I are one. As I walk back to the house, still caught in a kind of ecstasy, I suddenly wonder — is this the same beauty that went into the Pietà, that love between mother and son? I possess Father for the first time. For the first time he is mine. For this little hour there is no Mother between us, and I am transfigured by glory.

I go in to rouse the household.

CHAPTER 13

Freedom and Marriage Renewed

HEN OUR youngest child becomes engaged, a friend tells us, "Now you can do what you want." Alec and I look at each other uneasily. It never occurred to us, or at least to me, that after conceiving our first child twenty-eight years ago, we had anything but duty ahead with intermittent pleasure and joy along the line. And in this house we would go on renting the top floor indefinitely. Strangers would be going up and down our hall stairs, particularly the Chinese tenants, softly tiptoeing and charming.

So what do we want? Alec has already stated firmly to me that he's through with all parties of psychoanalysts or other professionals in that field. They never talk about anything except work and themselves and each other's work. I am not to accept any more invitations. (I, who felt so proud to be admitted into their select company.)

I suggest that we look for a place in Lincoln, an almost rural suburb of Boston with lots of conservation land. We see a house high above Thoreau's Fairhaven Bay, we see seven acres of land with no house visible except far down the Sudbury River in Concord. We make an offer and in the dickering caused by another higher bidder, Alec has one of his terrible attacks of throat spasms. But why? Why now? Am I pushing him into this? He shakes his head.

86

"Do you really want to move into the woods and get away?"
"Yes!"

I call quickly and offer the raise that seemed impossible an hour before. We get the house! Alec can swallow again. His whole body relaxes. We had bought the Willard Street house ten years before at $11,500 and sold it to Archibald MacLeish for $40,000. Our new house, three years old, with seven acres, is $38,000. The Lincoln place will be perfect for us; country stillness again and clean, sootless air. No cellar or attic — five rooms now instead of fourteen.

Our daughter's wedding a week behind us, the movers to come tomorrow, we pack books all morning, dusting as we go, and take them to our new and empty house. It is immaculate. Nothing is movable but a cake of soap and a roll of toilet paper.

We unpack the two cars full of cartons, put the books in some order in the plentiful shelf space, stack the empty cartons in the cars again and, limp and tired, sit ourselves on the bare floor with our backs against a bare wall. Alec takes out the third of a gallon of martinis left from the bridal party, two glasses, and an ice bucket. We sit uncomfortably and drink and dream and plan and congratulate ourselves. We start to soak in our new life.

Suddenly it is dusk.

"Alec, I'm drunk!" And I am, for the first time in my life. Alec leads me out to my station wagon.

"I'll follow you." And I know the labor of Sisyphus all the way to Cambridge. The car wanders back and forth over our long gravel road until we reach macadam with a white line. Determination plus now. I must not let the white line go away from the left front wheel. I stray to the left, to the right, but I never fully cross that dear white line. Where I leave it among the Cambridge streets, the car and I and the road are far harder to synchronize. But at last I find myself at our front door. And that's all I remember.

Now I'll be back in the country again, free like the child I once was. No one to see me, no dirty city air, no houses to look at — only the woods and river and minutiae of changing seasons with their gifts.

I have everything now. I never realized I needed isolation — homesick all these years. Here, too, we don't lock doors or pull shades. (We don't even have shades to pull.) No one ever gets this far down the back road. Keep everything wide open.

Alec and I settle down to a new kind of courtship; one on each end of a large two-handled saw, we widen the view of the river and Fairhaven Bay. All is well.

I don't even pause for the menopause. I occasionally get wonderful genital sensations that have been missing for so long. They delight me. We're both working. Alec has three new acting groups to play with and he has created the perfect workshop out of the two-car garage. We abandon the two-man saw and Alec buys a chain saw and clears the dense woods selectively. I push mightily at the tree as it begins to waver. It tips, going, going, then it crashes. Though I have always detested loud noises and violence, we're pleased, we're proud.

Before we go out to a party, Alec stands watching me as I sit at the lovely dressing table he has made, with my great-great-grandfather's collection of shells under glass before me. I'm wearing my brassiere, my corselet, my garter-fastened nylons as I do a job of light makeup. Alec says, as usual with a grin, "Go to the party just like that." He always wants me in beautiful clothes, except when I'm working. I find models' dresses in Filene's Basement. But he is so totally unselfconscious about his own appearance that he never buys anything but tools.

Often after supper, kitchen orderly, we sit in our two matching chairs before the fire — Alec with his left hand able to draw out the *Oxford Unabridged* and the *Crossword Dictionary* for our continual Double-Crosstic solving (while he finds the dictionary word, I go by hunch), or we turn on the new television with the blab-off switch he has built to wipe out all advertisements by the pressure of a thumb. Often he picks up a symphony on the hi-fi and, first sitting forward, then standing, he leads the full orchestra with intensity and significant, imperative gestures. He, Alec, the maestro, in identification with Munch, or Koussevitzky, or Fiedler, controlling motion, sound, pitch, nuance, and unity. Funny that that action should be so free and swift and his dancing be so little-boy-dancing-school rigid. In waltzing he never did learn the rhythm. Often, on such evenings, I go put on my pet indulgence — a black, transparent chiffon nightgown with the skirt cut almost in a circle and appliqués of black lace in appropriate places. For while I can't mentally hear music, I feel it, my body flowing to the rhythm. I move back and forth across the big room, watching my reflection in the long curved windows made mirrorlike by night. And I dance the dance of the maenads, or the vestal virgins, or other mad, passionate women, or serene goddesses, or blithe spirits, or new rock 'n' roll with tormenting, seductive hip-thrusting devilment, and he sits there lost and grinning.

When we are out in public I find amusement in spotting a gorgeous pair of undulating hips or some beautiful legs, or voluptuous breasts, and point them out to him. It is a kind of secret little game we have with each other.

I am amused that at a party where he sees a new attractive female he makes a beeline for her. I can see him talking his head off. Usually as we leave, she comes up to speak to me — warmly but looking a little puzzled. "You've got the most amazing husband. He spent the entire time talking about you and how wonderful you are." This is not the usual society gambit.

One day Alec puts down his magazine and says, "Go move that vase six inches to the right." I do. *Mirabile dictu!* He's quite right. I always thought he had no taste, like his mother. And now I study him again and see that the sadistic lift to the corner of his upper lip has completely gone — he can summon up a loving or amused smile and he rarely stutters. He no longer fusses until he finds his cigarette lighter, wallet, or car keys.

Does Isabelle sense Alec's increased security? For whatever reason, Alec, much more relaxed with me, is snappish toward his mother. At home there are no children with their unpredictability. I've told them to call before they drop in or to give notice if they want a meal or anything. So Alec has me to himself again, his new groups to act with, a new audience for his stories, new terraces to build; he is a man with his own acres. We can look at each other and know that there is love there. He drinks too much but he's not an alcoholic, I know, because he never touches the stuff before noon.

Isabelle, saddened and muted by poverty, is still correcting Alec or making suggestions. Nastiness that used to come my way has been transferred to her son and it makes me sad. I open all his mother's letters and read to him only the pleasant parts.

One day when Isabelle and I are momentarily alone, she turns to me almost pleadingly. "I don't understand Alexander. I try to be nice but he's so rude and contradictory and ugly. It's breaking my heart." She accepts my invitation for the next day, when, seated in an alcove of a silent club dining room, she reiterates her complaints. And in them there is far greater sadness than anger. She has lost all her money and she has lost her son and she has lost a lot of courage.

It is only as I talk that I know by sudden insight what I need to say, right or wrong. I tell her that Alec is not really mine. He has always been aware of and close to her in his feeling. He *is* hers. (I carefuly omit the word "love.") He is as dependent upon his mother as he was as a small child, wanting her approval. He is still trying to grow up and he handles his feelings of insecurity by getting angry and then disagreeable. But as a mid-fifty-year-old even the slightest devaluation or remark of hers in correction, reproof, or disapproval upsets him terribly. He wants the clean love of a mother who longs to see her son as perfect but has had to accept the fact that he is not Jesus.

"Can't you see? He's yours. He always has been yours and will be yours in the depths of his personality as long as he lives. He's tied to you. Why can't you see that he's yours?" There is no lie to this. He is still tied to his mother.

The change in Isabelle is immediate. The magic has worked. She relaxes. She has already begun to search for love in her aging and I have seen her far more caring of Dr. Robey. In her letters I have become "Harriet Dearest" and gratitude is expressed for the pleasure we have brought into her and Hal's lives. It's as if I have given the greatest gift of all and I can afford that gift from my heart. Her mouth is now almost sealed against her critical thoughts and she is not astute enough to hear the other very subtle message. In his true loving, giving, trust, and adoration Alec is mine and always will be. Oh, the wonderful magic of words. Now Isabelle is welcoming and pleasant and so Alec himself becomes more relaxed. It is a miracle that makes an old woman happy.

CHAPTER 14

The Children Marry—Empty Nest

ONE SUNDAY while Alec is out splitting wood and I sit in the big armchair that looks down the river, an incredible hunger or emptiness comes over me. Yet here I am with everything. Classical music comes from the fancy iron grill below the ceiling. I'm chain-smoking, on my second Scotch and soda, nibbling on my favorite Stilton cheese. Comfort, food, alcohol, nicotine, music, view, solitude, and peace. And Alec's happy. What the hell's the matter with me then? I'm still starved. Anxiety becomes so great it picks me right up out of my chair. I pace. Is this all there is? The emptiness resolves into loss and grief. With the last child gone there is freedom. Freedom for what?

Alec is creative and content, and he now has me. He so possesses me that if I gaze dreamily out the window for a moment or look vaguely into myself, he says, "Come back" or "Where *are* you?" I can't even think my kind of thoughts until he's asleep. I *have* to be free.

Is he trying to eat his way into my innermost soul by nibbling away at it? But nobody is going to possess that privacy. I think of it as my Mona Lisa, a mystery I myself don't know. Empty of children. Isn't this a time of crisis?

I recalled the different weddings of the four children. Alec had a good time at each one. During the engagement period he took the couple aside and told them how awful marriage is during the first ten years. "Make up your minds to put up with it, for you're going to go through hell." He left the girls in tears. I was hurt and I was furious, not so much by what he said as the way he said it, like his Jehovan grandfather. Shouldn't I have shut him up with constructive words, opposed his dire omens?

At all four bridal dinners Alec made his expected speech, the same stories that gave me shivers of resignation and amusement. While his varied accents were perfect, he loved most the "down-East."

After me an' Mariah got hitched at church, Ah git the hoss, Nellie, an' Ah sez ta Mariah, "Git up." An' she climbs up on the hoss. Ah git on an' we staat out ta ma faam. On the way the hoss stumbles. Ah sez, "That's oncet." We go on 'nuther mile or so an' Nellie (that's the hoss) stumbles agin. "That's twicet," Ah sez. Jes' as we wez comin' inta the barnyaad, Nellie (that's the hoss) stumbles a thurd time. Ah sez ta Mariah, "Git off." So she gits doun off an' whilst she's astandin' they-uh, Ah gits ma shotgun out of the kitchen an' shoots the hoss dead. Mariah, she stets to raant an' rave an' yell an' scream an' carry on sumpin' fierce. Ah doan' say nuthin'. Whin she's simmaa'd doun a bit an' stops fuh breath, Ah looks her right in the eye an' sez, "That's oncet!"

Another story had a different twist.

An artist with paints and easel was looking for the perfect New Hampshire scene. He found it — remote mountains, a lake, a field sloping down to the water's edge, and cows scattered around nibbling grass. He climbed the stone wall, set up his easel, and was hard at work when he heard a snort and then a roar behind him. He turned. A bull was charging him. Dropping everything, he bounded for the wall, the bull after him. He dove over just in time and stood there gasping and shaking. Farther down the field was a farmer sitting on a stool and rhythmically milking a cow. The artist walked down the outside of the wall until he was opposite the farmer and called, "Hey, how come that bull chased me and never bothered you?" "Oh, he don't mind me," was the reply. "He knows I'm milkin' his mother-in-law."

At each wedding I smiled charmingly and wept inside at the hurt that will be given and taken, the unhappiness to come to my darlings. But they weren't "mine" anymore. They were grown-up, independent, strong-minded, loving babes — how much food and caring to swell them from eighteen inches of helplessness to over six feet of power? I no longer have an essential part in this great furtherance of the race. Yet still I feel like an Earth Mother. All right, I'll raise turnips in the garden plot and so, maybe, become wise.

You, my daughter. Must I see you only superficially that I may not feel your marriage pain or interfere mistakenly in your new growth, or will you allow me to help without binding you in any way? And you, my sons — I still am Mary, the mother, the lover, who after a certain age pushed you off my welcoming lap, for you, too, could not relax but must squirm away from any prolonged physical contact as too dangerous, all three boys instinctively unwilling to be my Christ child. With you I never suggest anything. But I can help your wives, who are now my daughters. Help, when asked.

But not all marriages are unhappy, so play it clean, you kids. I'm glad to have you go. You're too big for me now and you nip at my teats. And if I wish to suffer, I can worry about you just as well, perhaps better, with you gone as when you were part of us.

I know now my emptiness — the barren womb (or perhaps a symptom-free menopause?). Let me then fertilize my mind. Let me create again.

"Alec, do you hear?"

He comes in with his arms full of oak.

"Dearie, how about a new project? Let's build something — start out in a baby way and make it grow into something beautiful. Use your imagination."

He lays and lights the fire, sits down and says, "Swimming pool."

"But we have the beach all summer. Would we use it that often?"

"You forget I'm here during the week. Besides, when your mother dies, and it shouldn't be long now, we're done with the beach. You won't have that family compulsion to visit her every day."

Inside I groan. No salt water. No sea smells and sounds. No familiar bumpy little foot paths, no flowing back to my beginning — born there in the summer and back every summer since. All life on earth has salt in its physical makeup. I *need* the sea. I'm of the sea. It is my tranquilizer as well as my wholeness.

CHAPTER 15

Deaths Come Fast

NOW COMES a period of deaths; Uncle Tom first, at age eighty-six, in Rhode Island. I have visited him often, for I now hold a tender relationship with him. My last memory of him is in a hospital bed, white and frail. It is a few days before Christmas in 1953. I bring two saucy little angel ornaments to hang on his bedstead. He looks and says testily, "Take them down and get them out of here." I do.

In his will, besides certain special bequests, he leaves all to his nieces and nephews. One of those bequests is $50,000 for me. When shown this by the executor, I cry a bit — from very complicated emotions.

One day Puss Leaman calls me to see if I will come to Hopkinton. He is selling his last cottage at auction and that includes his antiques. He wants me to pick out whatever I'd like because of his esteem for me. Oh boy, what a chance!

First he let his car and chauffeur go and then he gave up his apartment building. Then he sold the camp at Lake Umbagog, let the guides go, sold the huge and beautiful 1761 house in Hopkinton, the big old barn containing twenty cows and the new milking machines, and the various farmhouses, and has taken himself to the smallest one where he put his best furniture. Now he takes the train to Boston daily and sits in a small rented office, more erect, pink-cheeked, white-haired, and saintly than ever. And now every last thing goes to buyers except for what I take.

He welcomes me with a cup of black and bitter coffee. Proudly he explains his economy and efficiency: he makes coffee in that old white-speckled blue coffee pot by adding one tablespoonful of ground beans each morning and then boiling it with the earlier grounds of the last many days. When the pot becomes too full for more water, he rinses and starts again. I gather the longer he reboils the grounds the more bitter the coffee becomes.

He shows me through every room, three downstairs, two tiny ones up. His antiques are absolutely beautiful. I've always admired them at Thanksgiving or other gatherings. "Take any one thing you want," he repeats.

I hesitate. What would he like me to have? Does he really care? I hesitate too long, vacillating between a highboy and a desk and still looking around with hungry eyes.

"Ha!" he says, "I know what you want." He takes down from the wall a framed photo of George Angier Gordon. "He married you, remember?" Do I remember! The wink rushes back from my wedding day. Maybe I was then seeing life as a monstrous joke. He takes a piece of newspaper and wraps up the picture as if it were a Gutenberg Bible, goes out, lays it in the back seat, and I am apparently dismissed.

I drive home, gleeful inside with wry laughter at the jack-in-the-box surprise that came about in the flick of a lamb's tail.

George Angier Gordon does not arrive home with me.

Poor Puss. He takes up residence at the Algonquin Club and there his dignity and impressive appearance allow him to run up a huge bill. Or perhaps they reduce the rates. There he dies in 1953. Of what? I never remember what people, outside the immediate family, die of or from. They're dead. That's all. He leaves everything to Alex in a very simple will. In his club room we find frayed but beautifully laundered shirts, five well-worn Dunne suits, neatly pressed and carefully hung. Scanty underwear. Not one thing of monetary value. He has a storeroom in Frazier and Walker's and Alec and I go there, properly accredited. In his cold and barnlike space stands a large and lovely picture of his great-aunt done by Pratt in 1847, and a small suitcase in which I find an antique gold bracelet beautifully chased, perhaps belonging to that very aunt. I appropriate this for myself. And for the rest — heavy cardboard boxes labeled "Dunne" — all empty. Those famous suits! Could it be that they symbolized the peak of his personal success?

Alec and I drive home in silence.

But our children mourn his loss. He was simple and good with them, and taught them probity.

In 1953 Isabelle wrote from the heart:

Dearest Cunck,

It is difficult as conditions go more and more into reverse to tell you how much your helpfulness means to us both and what unspeakable comfort you give to me — and this gratitude, of course, includes our dear Harriet, for without her loving interest we can't picture how dreary life would have become.

I wish you could understand the depth of my emotions and their great variety so that their gratefulness could be transformed into what they really mean.

Then Hal Robey dies, age eighty-five, struck down by a car as he was stepping off the curb. He quietly got himself up and into a taxi, quietly went to his doctor's office, was quietly taken to the hospital where his fractured hip was set, and later, after release, lying quietly in his own bed at home, he went quietly from an embolism.

A mild and gentle man, famous among his peers and students for his subtle and quaint humor — a humor not seen at home. Was he Saint Hal or wasn't he? Was he a man or a mouse? In any case he was very happy that two of his grandsons were doctors.

Alec wept hard and bitterly. He knew a deep loss, the loss that comes from never having really known a father.

Isabelle visited us for a few days of adjustment. No repining or complaining and though she looked white and languid she remained businesslike. One day sitting on the sofa by the fire, she spoke suddenly, "I have just enough money to last me three years, then I will die."

She shows Alec her unwitnessed will, made impressive by her characteristic strong black calligraphy. After stating there was practically nothing to leave, after announcing a few bequests, particularly to Sandy — her portrait, her parents' portraits, Hal Robey's grandfather clock — she adds, "Use, distribute, or junk as you choose . . . don't let my death interfere with any pleasant plans you have made . . . none of this is binding and nothing is morbid. I appoint my son, Andrew Alexander Robey, sole executor without bond."

She now had to leave her Commonwealth Avenue house. In Stonington she rented, furnished, the servants' quarters of a huge mansion; these had been made over into an attractive, small, winter residence. She would have sold all her furniture, but I insisted that she save just enough for a small apartment in case she ever wanted to come back to the city. Katy stayed on with her.

We bought her a television set for her new quarters in spite of resistance. Later she wrote:

Dear Cunck,

It is high time that Harriet and you were truly thanked for the television which I definitely did not want but from which I now get much pleasure. Last evening, for instance, there was Douglas Edwards and the News, half an hour of the circus, The $64,000 Question, and The Highway Patrol. Of course if there weren't hours for reading during the daytime I should discipline myself, for nothing can take the place of good books. I am deeply and in a way intelligently grateful for your thoughtful provision.

Incidentally, do you like Sibelius?

We visited her frequently in Connecticut. That great tragic woman's finest moment came about three months before her death, when we were sitting around the dinner table. She said suddenly, "I was very cruel to you when you were first married. I'm sorry." And she went on rapidly to something else. I was stunned. I could not even say, "Thank you." That she had known in the back of her head all those years! That she could speak at this point! That she was making peace with someone, somewhere, somehow! Herself?

What happens to the proud, the neurotic, the narcissistic when they feel powers failing and instinct warns them of the coming end? If they are brave they speak, and Isabelle Robey was always brave when she made up her mind.

That summer she seemed much more frail and she stated she wanted to move back to Boston. To be nearer us?

Now the stored furniture is a godsend. Alec and I find a ground-floor apartment close to and as nearly like the Commonwealth Avenue house in arrangement as possible; shady street and elms in front, sun in the back, living room in front, dining room in back; in between, the bathroom, two bedrooms, one for her and one for Katy. We get in some plants and make the house as attractive as possible. Working madly, Alec and I have every last thing done — the old curtains fitting, fortunately, the three family portraits hung, the few ornaments arranged almost as they had been — and we brought back the few treasures she had given us when she moved away.

I've finished the last touches and am lying on the window seat, grateful to be there because of intense back pain of unknown cause, when Alec arrives from Connecticut with his mother, Katy, and their possessions. Isabelle walks in . . . Oh,

I did want her to be pleased! She looks into the living room, into her bedroom, just off the front hall, sees the windows opening onto a small blind alley giving light to the twin apartments, and cries out, "It isn't safe!" I remember she had always been terrified of rape, even to the point of locking her car and taxi doors whenever she rode in the city. We show her the strong iron bars.

Then she comes again into the living room, picks up the telephone, calls her two old best friends, and announces, "I'm back."

Then she is very, very tired and Katy tucks her into bed, and when we go in to kiss her and say we will be back the next day, she says, "Thank you, it will do nicely." Did she ever call her two friends again?

Two months later she is dead — almost three years to the day when she made her prophecy. It is five in the morning when Katy calls, and Alec can only say, "Thank God, thank God." The cancer that caused her no pain — indeed, she spoke of none, although the doctor kept her on medication — simply made her more and more quiet. Did she know? She had been right. There is no money left, not enough for a funeral and not enough for faithful Katy. Actually there is nothing but the things we had gotten out of storage and the green metal file box she always kept close to her, locked.

An extraordinary woman! All thoughts of approaching death, which of course she knew enough to know about, she kept to herself and quietly waited. She had requested that all the furniture in Katy's room be given to her and she regretted she had no money to leave her. We gave Katy the furniture and $700 — and she departed understandably angry, stating that she knew Mrs. Robey had her file box full of stocks and bonds and bankbooks. She had seen them. We paid for the funeral Isabelle had asked for and buried her beside Hal in the Connecticut graveyard.

Our four children divided up the rest of the furniture and the portraits. We kept an Italian plaster statue of Saint Cecilia (which she was very fond of and thought was the Madonna) and her flat silver — Tiffany's, of course — to save for future weddings of grandchildren.

The green file box? So nearly empty! No clippings, no photos, no mementos, no mention of family, no formal will but the copy of the one she had given to Alexander several years before. But there in their loneliness were the promissory note from Puss Leaman for $100,000, the pathetic little $100 prize for the best examination in applying to law school in 1896, two letters from her father, two from six-year-old Alexander to his grandpapa, a foreclosed mortgage on the Commonwealth Avenue house, and a bankbook and checkbook showing a total of $300.

She left no history whatever. Did she discard with bitterness or regret every single other thing connected with her husband, her ancestors, her friends? Was it only the intellect that mattered? Oh, the pity, the pity of it! I see her longing for love and her inability to be tender enough to ask for or to give it lest it be refused. Yet she agonized in a most dramatic style over every slight illness or serious condition of a friend of hers, any friend. Her emotions were almost stylized, but she was a good woman according to her lights. And she was able to change and soften. Hungry she was, always hungry. The something holy that lies between mother and son had been aborted and that was the tragedy of these two lives.

We had a quiet burial in the Connecticut town where her stone was already placed beside Dr. Robey's, and from that moment on Alex never had another attack of his acute indigestion.

As for me, I had been, for years, grateful for my unearned whiplashings. They enabled me to find that I could not be diminished unless I let it happen.

Was Isabelle Robey a social climber? I don't think consciously. It was bred in her to do the right thing according to the best society of the day. How else had her papa gained his eminence? Her very powerful personality with the masculine edge to it, her swift attachment to intelligent or creative people, her "good works," her prematurely snow-white hair, her handsome face and carriage and brilliant couturier clothes, and her reputation as the best dinner partner in the city carried her up far. As far as she wanted?

So I was to be properly trained also. Who "got" me into the Sewing Circle of 1918–1919 or into the Junior League, both after my marriage? I never knew enough to ask. Was Isabelle's hand in that, too?

Puss Leaman *was* a pusher. He had files and files on everyone he ever met socially or on business, with the interests, the income if known, the travels, family members, social position, and other vital statistics of each individual. These he perused often, and frequently added more people — up to the point where his name disappeared from the tongues of men.

I sit by Mother, so slight in the double bed, and I wait. The nurse has said it would be very soon now, so I send her down to have coffee until I call her. Death is the third actor in this room.

For Mother has gradually faded since Father died, nine years ago. She would have some angina when she could find nothing to change or renovate, nothing to keep her mind and body active. Small strokes were increasing, each assault lessening her. As they became more and more frequent and she more and more an invalid and more paranoid, we installed nurses. As time passed, she accused all those who attended her of primitive infantile actions. I was called in to help and I could see how her mind had gone too far to have judgment and control, and that she was living so far back in infancy she accused the nurses of things small children do and that probably she herself had once done. So the household all stayed, with perhaps more compassion. It always amazes me that, as I mount the stairs to visit her and hear her screaming in rage at her attendant and I enter the room, some remaining power grabs hold — her face becomes serene and normal. She always greets me with, "Here's my darling girl!" And she holds my hand and by and by tells me quietly of the rats she hears in the walls. She's too ashamed even now to let a child of hers see her out of control.

I sit there. She is going, going. My fingers are on her pulse, which is faint and erratic. I tell her of my love for her, how wonderful she is. For has she not endured with patience a life where depression lay upon her shoulders in her own atonement of some sin?

In sudden insight I gained understanding of the sweetness of her character — see no evil, speak, hear, and do no evil. Repentance all her life? Neuralgia most of her life, low-grade depression, and her unconscious mind driving her to do and say things she didn't see or know. She gave all for others, asking so little for herself. She would buy nothing for pleasure as if she didn't deserve any gratification.

Darling Mother, in her lifelong battle. Never could she be truly herself. Until Grandmother's death, Mother was tied to her, following her summer and winter, seeing her practically every day. What mysterious obligation was she under?

What is passing now between us, Mother and me? Is not some communication made? I murmur my love which is both existential and primordial. What is happening as that pulse weakens? We are two good, kind, and loving women. Yet the Mona Lisa in me speaks to the Mona Lisa in her. It is tempting to run away fast or ring for the nurse — move into immediacy and activity. No, unknown things are happening and I must feel them, my fingers on her pulse.

Now she's gone. I sit a moment or two to accompany her on

the first part of her journey, whatever that may be, but take my hand from hers as I sense a light coolness in it, and I pull up the covers as if to keep her warm, and I say, "God bless" and ring for the nurse.

And as I stand there, hearing the feet hurry up the stairs, the crazy old poem comes, "Mother, may I go out to swim? Yes, my darling daughter. Hang your clothes on a hickory limb, but don't go near the water." And now I will no longer go to the beach for the summer.

Why does love have to be so confusing? Was this her last message to me? Or her first? What price beauty of soul?

With all parents gone Alec and I become the older generation. We can no longer look up or down on them nor they on us. We are we and the young are watching. Also, we're next. Our time is coming. We've nothing to feel guilty about except the past. I'm fifty-eight, Alec sixty — not so old. We *feel* old and begin to fuss about our bodies and to wonder, vaguely, when. How fast are we going to wither? Isn't it our choice?

Analysis taught me what my unconscious was up to and the games I was playing. Social work gave me the broad intellectual understanding of the activities of the psyche. What now?

CHAPTER 16

Professional and Personal Heights

STAND on the top of Mount Katahdin, an isolated 5,268 feet — tremendous to me who never climbed before. The air blows clean from the far-off sea. I fling out my arms and breathe deeply, feeling mighty and eternal, for I am well again.

Six years before, in 1956, I had fractured a vertebra which early X-rays didn't disclose. The doctor was an old friend of Hal Robey's and almost violently opposed to the new back operations. Treatment was conservative: two or three weeks of hospital bed rest with hot packs, physiotherapy, a brace, then home — and this repeated over and over through the years. The last brace was a quite horrible iron contraption — worse than the one I wore as an adolescent — to keep my back rigidly straight. It only increased the pain sharply. I had to wear it every time I stepped from bed.

It was in that pain I saw the two mothers through their deaths; within that pain I worked as chief social worker at a small children's agency, constantly half-nauseated even though sitting in a folding lawn chair at the job. With that pain I finally could no longer go on, and out of it I called in our two doctor sons. "Do something — I've had it!" Because of the pain I saw Dr. Murray for a while to understand if it held psychosomatic elements. He said no, except for my anger and tension at the pain.

And finally I started writing desperately, out of pain, whatever — free-associating as I had in analysis years before. And what did I write? Agony columns while Alec was at work or I was bed-bound, or when I woke abruptly in the middle of the night.

Those free-associative, swift-jotted, and despairing ramblings which held me steady during the years of pain, and at which I now look, appalled, are so full of emotional writhings, murderous rages, and primitive imagery that they could only be excused by the average person under the cloak of "insanity." For what, so graphically, I describe doing to others goes back to the time of man's first conscious awareness (so symbolically told in Genesis), a time when to kill or deliberately inflict intolerable pain gave the giver no pain whatever. And since this was my own writing, this then is what is latent in me. Better and better do I know the worst and most primitive in me.

In Greek mythology, the gods and goddesses went merrily along with the eye for an eye, tooth for a tooth principle and committed every type of crime, violent retaliation, or foul brutishness. Mythology seemed all so clean — being nicely removed from reality. As are all myths, and often they are fun and funny because no one feels remorse, no one carries responsibility. The old Greek plays, based on the actions of the gods, stirred and excited, but left the audience innocent.

I wondered why prolonged pain produced such helpless rage. Because you *are* so helpless. (Hear the anguished scream of a deserted infant.) Or you are the now angry Earth Mother who could be holding an apple or an atomic bomb while saying, "Let them fall. Wipe them out. They are unworthy." Come the flood.

My sons referred me to the Peter Bent Brigham Hospital, where we started on the old routine. It's too bad a quietly controlled woman has to howl or sob or cry or abandon her dignity to make a doctor change his emotional distance glasses for a bifocal approach in which intractable pain is seen as it affects the particular patient.

I broke down, quite shamefully — yet shamelessly — one day, and then things moved. A myelogram was done, a laminectomy performed, and during the operation it took a long time to pick out the many pieces of disintegrated disk from the nerve canal. In a short time I was home.

Now wanting more than the repetitious classical back exercises, I found a physical trainer with a gymnasium, his clients mostly athletes. Twice a week I worked to my limit. Each visit included a shower and a long, deep massage.

It's summer. I feel thoroughly vibrant and social work is calling. A letter arrives from Boston University School of Social Work asking me to teach second-year casework full time (to me the choicest of assignments) and I could at last *be* somebody, a Professor! Alec is not helpful when he says, "Do what you want." So what do I want?

There's a simple little boarding inn on Lake Winnipesaukee not far from Dr. Murray's summer cottage. I formerly stayed there overnight if I got into an emotional jam during his vacation and I needed a couple of interviews. This inn had good country food cooked by Mrs. French and you ate what was on your plate when it was brought in from the kitchen, you slept on a rather sagging iron bedstead and there was one bathroom for six rooms. I find it the same. I get my old front room in the Annex only a few feet away from the rocks that edge the shore, and on the tiny porch just outside is the same old Gloucester hammock with red cushions. Here I sit for three days, looking out at the lake, occasionally taking a walk or picking wildflowers for a tumbler on my bureau. I knit and think and float and periodically jot in a notebook; one section is written "Pro," another is "Con." I don't think about what I write but simply record every association to the job offer.

Since I leave early tomorrow I now read what I have written.

The waves are lip-lapping on the rocks and the late summer dusk is moving in. First the "Pro" list. Summarized, it offers professorship, aggrandizement, power, learning and teaching (which I love), authority, recognition, and attestation as a person. Maybe my extended WASP family would look twice. Next the "Con" list: nights of meetings, traveling to conferences, concern with labor relations or with certification, getting involved with school work policy and other unknown responsibilities. And I as a person, still shy, am an ivory tower escapist. I want only to do the best casework possible. Most of the older famous social workers I know are single women with lives dedicated and directed into one path, the creative self-sacrificing professional with no room for a husband.

There's no question. Alec's name stands out bold and strong as his signature. I am a wife and mother who works. Suddenly I laugh at these wishful dreams of glory and go home to Alec without thinking where the sacrifice lies or if there is one. I only know that truth within me has spoken. Meek little Harriet, to become Professor Robey? What a joke! I am simply a social worker and my agency and my clients are my job.

Dean Conant is very annoyed at my refusal of his plum, for who with any common sense would reject it? I'm offered the same by the Simmons School of Social Work, but again I decline unless I can work half-time. But that is not enough for them.

An incident occurs which delights and enlightens me. The doctor-director of a Boston clinic wants me on his Board of Trustees. He knows I will be socially acceptable to them and that I can interpret the goals and activities of the clinic treatment in simple descriptive words. I'm told that after considerable discussion the board voted me down. "She's betrayed her class by becoming professional." I'm pleased. I understand even more clearly where certain lines lie — social lines, professional lines, snob lines. And still I'm concerned to be only myself as Alec's wife, my children's mother, and a worker-provider in an area my personality is best suited to, the depth of humanness and humanity rather than width. Not the executive nor the activist nor the militant for me. And I hate long-argued meetings.

In August I accept an invitation from our son and his family, which includes four small children, to go with them to Baxter State Park in Maine for a week and to climb Mount Katahdin. Our lodging is Twin Pine Camp, deep in wilderness. On the day of the climb we drive to base camp and start up — a twenty-mile hike. My son backpacks the youngest, my daughter-in-law helps push the smallest of the three daughters up stone ledges where the iron handholds are too far apart for her reach.

At last we stand at the top. The feeling that I almost floated up the difficult climb was extraordinary in its euphoria. And whatever way I turn, my eyes go their limit of vision and then withdraw before the enormousness and endlessness of space.

Mountains are magic, I find. While we eat bag lunches, I tell the four tired little ones of the secret entrance near us at the top; it leads down a staircase from which doors open into rooms full of wonderful and different toys — a tiny airplane that really flies . . . a doll that really talks . . . magic power to become any size wanted — and the children excitedly add to what I might have missed. And as we go down in imagination there are more and more treasure rooms. At the very bottom center of the mountain are two rooms, one full of jewels and gold and silver, all shiny and beautiful and precious, all hidden from sight to humans unless they can find the key to the door and the daring. The other room, I tell them, is full of dark and angry feelings that are like bad and evil spirits. They can look into that room when they're older and ready, for in there is the wisdom of the world.

My grandchildren sit enraptured.

We assemble to start down. I take a final look to the east and to the Atlantic and know this is the first spot in the United

States that the sun touches as we roll eastward to welcome it. My longing for space and distance and wide openness is momentarily satisfied. I am no longer ill and old. I have mastered. I long for the so-distant sea. That only is missing for me.

When we finally reach the dry watercourse with its boulders, I find my legs are uncontrollable jelly. I have to ask my son for his arm.

Mount Katahdin, once thrust up in fire, is eroded to a flat top through the millennia. And I, sixty-two, formerly an invalid, have climbed the enduring natural symbol of pride, beauty, and permanence.

I have mastered it, now I can go on.

CHAPTER 17

The Sea Calls, the Storm Smashes

HE SEA calls. Even with our swimming pool outside the bedroom door, exactly egg-shaped and so pleasant for floating in the middle, it's the salt I cry for and for our whole family compound where I grew up and where I have spent at least a part of every summer since.

My boastful pride at the top of Mount Katahdin went too far. My challenge was heard to the last closed room deep beneath and the gods of darkness growled and stirred. I go blind with my own desires. I *must* have the sea.

I'm told of a gem of a little houseboat — a superstructure on a flat-bottomed two-ton river barge, all mahogany inside, a beautiful little English stove, two bunks, and a powerful outboard motor. Her name: *Zuleika Dobson* — Max Beerbohm's willful lady who drove all the Oxford students mad with longing. I look at it with Alec and I look to Alec.

Yes, I'm unreasoning and my argument is totally illogical. We can anchor it in the family cove at the beach and spend weekends on it; we don't need to go near the family, we can travel around Ipswich Bay, explore the Annisquam River, Gloucester, Rockport, or enter for the night any of the many little estuaries. Blind, arrogant little princess — or is it some devil that's tempting me, making the worse appear the better reason?

"All right," Alec says. I'd forgotten my power over him and when that permission comes, I buy the boat fast.

A son and I bring *Zuleika Dobson* across the bay. She takes the long low swells with a comfortable roll. We tie her up to a huge granite mooring block with its long heavy line and buoy. Alec is to come down Friday before Labor Day when we'll quietly christen her. So on Wednesday I go to the shore to paint the superstructure and lay in food.

The wind has risen as I drive and the rain is raw and slatting. My children are all in their houses for the holiday and I go into one family house after another — all doors and windows wide open, great breezes rushing through. Raw. Damp. I'm cold and I want warmth and comfort and welcome and love. There's no one anywhere around in any house. Everyone, I find later, had gone to Halibut Point to watch the waves smash and shatter, for this storm has been belatedly labeled a hurricane.

So I'm hurt and mad. All right. I'll go out on the *Zuleika* and light a fire in the stove, curl up under the down comforter, and snooze. Being as one with a dinghy, I get into ours on the lee side of the small family pier and reach the houseboat, shipping only a little water from the now almost frightening waves. Inside, with the fire going and the comforter over me, I am certainly rocked in the cradle of the deep.

A horn sounds persistently. Finally I poke my head out of the companionway and a son, standing beside his car on the big breakwater pier yells, "You're dragging! Row over and get me!" I manage, though I ship more water and the waves are wicked, until I reach the lee of the long pier. My son rows back and we clamber up on the houseboat.

In my effort to lower *Zuleika Dobson*'s heavy anchor, I catch my foot in the mooring line. It gives one huge jerk in an extra-large wave and then another jerk. The rope has caught my ankle. Instinctively, I fold myself over the bow lines as my leg is dragged, crack, crack. My son, inside, running the motor now, drives full speed ahead and my foot is loosed. He rushes forward. "Ankle broken in two places. I heard it," I say to him.

"Crawl down into the cabin."

He grabs a heavy pillow and the elastic cord from the curtains around the head, and immobilizes my foot. "Back as soon as I can." But before he leaves I ask him for the comforter, the phenobarbital from the medicine cabinet, and the crossword puzzle. We're both very cool and collected.

Time passes. A long time passes. But finally my son returns with a motorboat that is large enough for the job and then it seems like more hours before he secures *Zuleika* with the two anchors and she is safe from the rocks. So at last I hitch myself down into the motorboat, my son holding up my leg. Other men in yellow slickers stand close at hand.

Now I can relax. I am on a mattress in the back of a station wagon which has been driven down to the beach. Now I am lying on a stretcher in the basement corridor of the local hospital, nurse and family standing around waiting for the X-ray technician, who, it seems, has gotten lost somewhere in town. I begin to shiver and ask for a blanket. I'm pleased that I do not go into shock. And surprised that no one should have thought I might be cold. A blanket is brought.

Ah, the X-ray man. Now into the X-ray room.

When I'm conscious again the orthopedic surgeon says, "You miscounted. Three breaks, not two."

But I feel good. As I had on Katahdin, now again I had battled nature's elements and won. But . . .

It was far worse than three broken bones. Operation followed operation before I was fully back together. The damage ran from the toes up to the backbone on the left side.

Now, no more beach. I go back to Lincoln, tamed. I give the boat to my son.

In between operations Alec and I take freighter trips. These, despite my pain, were adventures that suited both of us. And

Alec's retirement is coming up. Every month, on the sixteenth day, I have a special little dinner and drink to "one month less." Oh, how Alec has disliked his job all these years. His job and the patronage of the family. He'd been so faithful and dogged, so thoughtful of me in the hospital all those times, visiting with the mail but not sitting down to relax. He hated hospitals. Had I been punishing Alec? What the hell did he eat when I was hospitalized?

But never again would I look for excitement to soothe aloneness and cold and emptiness.

CHAPTER 18

The Many Marriages

*A*T LAST the day of retirement comes and Alec arrives home early from work, beaming. I've planned a big party — all our children and close friends, those who knew Alec's longing to be free from responsibility to business superiors. Every kind of liquor, every kind of hors d'oeuvre, and a succession of happy toasts with champagne.

When the time comes, Alec reads, with delight and dramatic emphasis, a schedule for retirement sent by a business friend. To me it's outright funny and every man listens avidly. Doesn't it hold an almost universal masculine cry? And the women? I can almost see them thinking, "Male chauvinist pig." The latest term of opprobrium.

The schedule is as follows:

7:00	Wake up and laugh at silent alarm clock which has been turned off the night before.
7:00–7:01	Brisk calisthenics while lying in bed.
7:01–9:00	Go back to sleep.
9:00–9:30	Debate whether to shave. Decide not to.
9:30–10:00	Read newspaper and have breakfast. Bourbon, toast, bacon, eggs, and coffee.

10:00–11:00	Give wife orders of the day, and point out her errors of the day before.
11:00–11:15	Coffee and bourbon break spent resting on sofa.
11:15–12:15	Front-porch rocking-chair session. Make plans on how to spend tomorrow in constructive way.
12:15–12:30	Highballs with next-door neighbor.
12:30–1:30	Lunch. Beer, beef sandwich, apple pie, and cheese.
1:30–1:35	Read good book to improve mind.
1:35–3:00	Nap on sofa.
3:00–4:45	Back-porch rocking-chair session to get benefit of the afternoon sun. Review morning's plans for tomorrow. Decide tomorrow is a bad day to start new project.
4:45–5:00	Inspect vegetable garden; point out to wife areas where she should do more hoeing.
5:00–8:30	Cocktail hour.
8:30–9:30	Dinner. Wine, sirloin steak, salad, mashed potatoes, gravy, and ice cream.
9:30–11:59	Discuss with wife why world is going to hell; lay out her schedule of work next day.
11:59–12:00	Write postcard to boss saying how much you miss the old office gang, and how you're champing at the bit to get back.
12:00–12:01	Go to bed with second good book of day to improve mind. Book drops to floor.
12:01	Fall asleep.

After the last guests leave, and the children have helped clean up, Alec looks at me with a loving, relaxed face and says, "My kitten!" and we lock up and we lock ourselves in each other's arms and his smell is that good, clean masculine smell, and his body is firm and warm.

Tomorrow morning the alarm will go off early for me. Why don't I stop working? He'd love that. This has been another choice. For it's now a new marriage again. He is to shop and learn his way around the stores and markets and spend hours working on accounts and do odd carpentry jobs and wait for twelve-thirty, when I arrive and get him some food. (This is a sore point in many marriages, giving rise to the saying, "I married you for better or worse, but not for lunch." And certainly some of Alec's eating habits have been a long-time irritation, though a minor one. At a cocktail party I used to stuff on all the unusual or special delicacies and neither wanted nor needed any more that evening — just go to bed. Whereas Alec would eat nothing, unless there were shrimp, and on the way home it always was, "What's for dinner tonight?")

I am now working half-time, eight-thirty to twelve, so I hurry home by twelve-thirty because we've cooperated. He has let me work so the rest of the time I give to him. He needs my company and he wants to be fed.

I look back over our forty-odd years of marriage, at the shifts in our joint lives. I see many marriages in a marriage and in my notebook I jot them down. Alec gets interested and adds to them.

1. A marriage born out of passionate joy and anticipation; a honeymoon where we gain a deeper knowledge of each other's personal habits, interests, and capacity to laugh.

2. Settling in to bread-and-butter days, each takes the gauge of the real other and the battle of the sexes begins. The first irritation can be as simple as the slight difference in the way one hangs up towels, or doesn't hang them up. And this carries over to practically every daily act. We are also dealing with our families. They watch our every move. They push and pull, each in its own pattern. I feel that Alec deserts me. He's changed.

3. The third marriage is when pregnancy begins and my mind and body are withdrawn, up to a point, from Alec. There's homemaking and job-making and both put new stress on us. With the childbearing and delivery, tension is high and the mothers-in-law watch and worry.

4. The fourth marriage comes when the children are most active and demanding. Now a woman changes from one who rolls on the floor with the children to one who is edgy and cross, being overwhelmed with her daily work and all the diapers of the children she has insisted on having (or he has, thoughtlessly). Confusion and "never getting ahead" have caught everybody in the family. His depression comes from worry over his ability to support so many. In this case, I, the woman, withdraw from or desert Alec. He should save me.

5. Our fifth marriage is when I enter analysis. Here, for a while, I really did desert Alec. I was changing before his very eyes. Choice: stay together or separate?

6. Marriage at the time of war is a different life, our minds being diverted from ourselves and there being no time for introspection. But again, in a way, I have deserted Alec in this sixth marriage because of my studying social work, a new, absorbing interest.

7. Then the children marry one by one — the nest is empty. During this seventh stage we have a choice. There's nothing to take our minds off each other's faults. We are once again two people living together, bonded, and knowing all each other's unpleasant idiosyncrasies. It's as if we looked at each other afresh. Do we like what we see?

8. Now all the parents have died. There may be grief or there may be relief. But we're the older generation — the next to go. A sobering thought. And yet, we still worry about the welfare of our tribe.

9. In the ninth stage I go through a lot of back pain, recover after an operation, and begin to feel immortal. I insist on having

my will. I get into more physical trouble. Yet, here is a more positive type of marriage. Alec doesn't reproach me, he stands by me, comforting and strong.

10. The tenth marriage is Alec's retirement. We're closer but in some ways nearer a breaking point. Too much togetherness. We settle down to a supposedly uninterrupted old age.

It becomes shockingly clear to me now how much I have run the show, doing or taking what I wanted and trying to make up to Alec in other ways. In each new crisis, over and over, he's had to shift gears for me. New orientation, new duties, new stresses, and, we hope, new growth. For in each of these "marriages" lie the potentiality for better or worse — for an emergence of heretofore hidden traits and impulses, or fast-growing rigidity of mind and body.

We are now more niggling and edgy. We, two, alone. Incompatibility is coming out in the open and shows up in little annoyances that, while they existed for years, were absorbed by larger issues. I've seen an ugly, tight look come and stay in some women's eyes after their husbands retire. These women have their lives well laid out in constructive and soul-satisfying activities, and to have a mate interfering with his need of a wife-mother-lover constantly beside him brings up a rage in women that has no outlet. So hate lies there behind the eyes, and the body moves without serenity into determined and aggressive home activities.

Is this happening to me? Do I love Alec too much? He loves and depends on me. We both sacrifice. And we join in finding new things to create.

CHAPTER 19

Communication

AT THE supper table one night, feeling the rigidity in my jaws to be tighter than usual, I say impulsively, "Dr. Robey, I need to talk to you." (That's a good start — Alec had wanted to go into medicine but could never pass chemistry.) "And please don't defend or argue or even answer. You're being Dr. Murray now for me."

He is obviously alarmed but says nothing. I go on with complaints. I might say, "Why the hell did you have to squeeze Mrs. Bryant's hand so hard? She's very arthritic. And it makes me furious when you use my car and forget to pull the seat forward or see that it's full of gas afterward and why can't you use the word love or ever kiss me and you snored all last night and —"

He opens his mouth —

"No." I cut him off. "No, don't do that. Just listen. *Please,* just listen. You'll get your turn." And before I'm through I can remember what piqued my anger.

It takes a little time to learn and I am careful not to overload him, but Alec gets the point. I finally wind down. Then I laugh. "I see now why I got mad at you," I say. "It's because of what happened this morning at the office," and I tell him.

Now the same game can go on with him. He starts, "Dr. Robey, I've got to talk."

Then he might tell me there is a faucet that I usually leave dripping. (I want to say, "Well, then put in a new washer," but I keep my mouth shut.) Or he says, "You forgot to fill your car with gas and you still quote your mother and you're always looking vague as if you weren't with me and the kids are here too much and your writing stinks." And I listen silently and intently and finally say, "Feel better now?" And he nods. And that is always our ending.

It turns out to be a lovely technique; no hard feelings; but instead we are communicating, albeit in a "your turn, my turn" way. But in all our marriages I've never directly attacked him. Now we are on common ground. Laughter returns.

Is this all there is? Isn't it enough? We're getting old. Retirement means you're done. Society says you can now begin to degenerate and disintegrate.

I can now laugh at the *et ux*, as I was, as wife, in the old legal papers. Alec and I are man and wife and we take our freighter trips and we go on building stone walls and though he's had two cataract operations and given up acting because of night driving, it's as if somehow he is at last himself, loved and loving. Gone are the florid ersatz letters sent with such genuine love in 1923, for now the adolescent passion has resolved itself into the clean and clear phrase, "My kitten!"

Alec's great gift to me is his giving me freedom to learn and grow no matter what my age. My gift to him is probably my deep caring and impulsiveness, which at least give him daring and life. So what if he couldn't or wouldn't recognize all his grandchildren? Why did he have to? (Of the fifteen, eleven were little girls all with gentle manners, long flaxen hair — loose or in braids — and a family resemblance. And he would look at them vaguely and say, "Oh, hello." And that was that. They were all in awe of him except for one, our daughter's oldest daughter, who could tease him or flirt with him winningly or even perch on his lap and he would grin sheepishly. Oh yes, he knew *her* name.)

Older, older, an eleventh marriage. Alec is now approaching his eighties. He has had one or two tiny strokes but all goes on as usual. Tender, lovely, and calm years. There is nothing more wonderful than his softened face. When he looks at me and says, "*My* kitten," something wonderful flows between us and fulfills me.

Even his drinking . . . why bother to fight about that at this age? I remember an older woman who came for help at our agency. She wanted a divorce, but it turned out she wanted a sympathetic listener to her complaints about the awfulness of her alcoholic husband and the dreadful things he yelled at her. She gloried in her suffering. But the glint in her eye showed her reason for living. She enjoyed the yelling and shouting matches and she always had the last word. Then the couple rested and he took out another six-pack and they went at it again. Did I, too, in my way, like being a victim?

Alec won't give up his three nightly drinks. His age, however, is complicating the effect of the alcohol. After dinner, after listening to music or a television program, he says suddenly, "Bedtime," and starts to rise. His legs give way totally. He is on the floor. Muscles will not synchronize. He cannot, neurologically, get his legs going because his muscles don't respond. So he struggles and struggles and then collapses exhausted — for only a moment — and then he starts again. He can't even get his shoulders up. I try a pillow under his head, a blanket over him, and say, "Relax, rest a bit, then try again." It's no use. Some force is driving him to stand up and be a man, a gentleman. Is he really drunk? I don't know. Maybe.

The situation is not without its comic aspects. With my bad back I must be respectful of lifting, yet between us I get him onto a scatter rug and by clearing a path along the floor of the living room to our bedroom, I haul the rug and Alec into bed. His sigh of relief is tremulous and tremendous. I help him off with his clothes. Now he has to have his pajamas on. Suddenly he comes to life and, with utmost precision, takes out both of his contact lenses and puts them neatly in their little cups.

It is my turn to sigh with relief. But I wish there were a snapshot of the two of us. He's a happy man and an old one, so why get angry? And next morning he always wakes up feeling fine. So now we're reaping the rewards for our tolerance.

I could not have anticipated Alec's death, for he seemed so much as usual. Only a few days before, he was out plowing with the jeep, ramming more snow into already big banks. Power! He still needs power. But . . .

CHAPTER 20

Widowhood

*L*ORD, hear our prayers of thanks for the life of Alexander Robey.

We give thanks for a man who overcame the rigid rod of childhood training and a discipline that withheld love as punishment for human error.

We give thanks for a spirit that would not be broken nor frozen but found ways to express itself, indirectly if need be, but nonetheless express itself in courage to stay with tasks that were less than fulfilling. With deep regard for family, with the wisdom to find a wife who could laugh at herself and bend her warmth to melt away rigid patterns learned in another climate, he had a lively and unique gift of perception and representation of many aspects of the human condition given expression on the stage. His was a poetic identification with nature that seldom was expressed but every so often found its way through in a reflective comment or silent pause.

Lord, we human beings are at once grand and foolish. We strive and stumble. But there is dignity in it. Thou hast placed dignity in our being which is most clearly seen at the end of a race faithfully run. We honor the dignity of Alexander Robey, a rigid uprightness with soft center and humble aspect. We honor the dignity of a man who ran his race and finished it. We give thanks for the mercy of its conclusion and for the quality it leaves in its wake.

Afterward a big party at our house, organized by the children. Then just family left, about twenty around the fire until midnight — close, loving, drawing into one and renouncing and reminiscing; never to be forgotten. This is the real service for Alec.

On Monday I'm back at work. But night after night I think and think, go through every stage of grief, anger, desertion, and panic and try to see what I am doing and what it means to be half a person. I have now entered into widowhood after fifty-two years of marriage, with a knife of hurt in my heart.

The end of a marriage — a marriage till death us shall part. Alone for the first time in an entire life! Bereavement. My emotional weathervane spins wildly and reverses under the cold gales of utter emptiness or the burning ones of overflooding emotion. Bewilderment. Fine reward for all my self-sacrifice. You took away half of me; give it back! The helpless infant screams its fear, rage, and pain.

I was a bad wife. I was a good wife. I made him happy. I drove him to drink. Something is dead in me. No, it isn't. There's unfinished memory.

There is no spring this year. I manage at work, my clients helping me as I help them. Nights are bad, but I make myself answer a few of the welcome sympathy letters.

My grief is not for him — he went as he would have wanted — but for myself. No place to lay my tired head, no way to assuage my hunger to be held or my need to nurture. I want to feel "rescued" by my sons. But hadn't I pushed them away physically as they grew that they might become free men, free of the Pietà tie? An inherited family code holds that you don't show misery with its subtle call for succor before your adult sons lest they become bewildered with their own reactions. And I'm afraid of the passionate intensity of my own tenderness and longing. And our — my — daughter lives in another state and a long telephone call is not a long, warm hug. Besides I want to be a "wonder woman," don't I? I want to master my woes.

One absolutely blind black despairing evening, I think of an article in the newspaper on Transcendental Meditation. The doctor who wrote it mentioned the mantra could be any word, such as *one*. Let's try it, I think, and I follow instructions as to belly breathing and end my long outbreath with the word *one*.

But the sound that comes out of me is *growth*. Who said that? I try again. The same result in spite of my determination to say "one." Then a gremlin that had been hiding so long within me begins to laugh. Is a good spirit guiding me or an evil one? But *growth* it will be.

The time comes when I draw the first breath, the first long breath of freedom. I can go and come at my will, sleep and wake early or late, eat what and when I wish, think my long, long thoughts, be joyous, angry or sad without constant concealment. Ha! I am free.

There's the other side of the coin, bitter. My protector has deserted me — forever. Bewildered, powerless, I watch things go into disrepair. Decisions, heavy to make. The children have different voices and their advice confuses me. Besides, I wouldn't be so free if I listened to them. Underneath is a whisper, "I'm so lonely." But I block it.

A leap into activity: I put our house on the market, make a down payment on a condominium in woods edging conservation land also in Lincoln, make plans to go to the beach again, at last! And I don't consult the children. I tell them.

And Alec had been laid tenderly where Mother lies, out of sight and sound in that sad, sweet place called Lethe, forty fathoms deep.

CHAPTER 21

The Back Strikes Back

I AM AT the beach at last after eighteen years of absence, with all the young helping restore and repair the old house, making it a joyful plunge into activity. I relive what the sea means to me. And had I not learned that through the continual motion of continents that little space of shore of mine was lifted each century by a few inches and pushed farther away from Europe by great forces within the earth, and that those billions of tiny white barnacles, moving with infinite slowness to another little space, scraped away at the granite rocks and eroded them year by year? This place was a microcosm and was I not, at every moment while there, aware inside of the changes in tides, reacting emotionally to the phases of the moon — that moon that dies so faintly silver white in the sky to a nothing but then is reborn fully, in another twenty-eight days, just as my own cycle, when it finally started very late, repeated faithfully the moon's timing. And always there is exploring among the rolls of straw and wrack, tossed high by storms, every crab carapace, every limpet shell, brittle pale sea urchins, bits of driftwood, sea pods, dried straw of marsh grass, transparent cream-colored baby horseshoe crabs; everything had had its own destiny as I had mine, of birth, life, and death.

But almost nightly as the sun sets, I walk across the field to the glacier-rounded ledge of lichened rock whence I look out and beyond or down below me to the sand and sea and the teeming life along the rocks. Here I do not think. Perhaps I am waiting for something. Sharply I remember back to a poem of sorts written at a time of desperation in the early years of our marriage.

I.
Let me not cry.
The moon is full. The land floats free.
I know that I can walk across the sea.
Along that silver path and with the tide . . .
No, I must turn my head aside
And hear the sea wind sigh.
Let me not cry.
I.

Here I was born and here I hoped I would die. Melville says in *Moby Dick:*

> Yes, as everyone knows, meditation and water are wedded forever. . . . Why did the old Persians hold the sea holy? Why did the Greeks give it a separate deity, and own brother of Jove? Surely all this is not without meaning. And still deeper, the meaning of that story of Narcissus, who because he could not grasp the tormenting, mild image he saw in the fountain, plunged into it and was drowned. But that same image, we ourselves see in all rivers and oceans. It is the image of the ungraspable phantom of life; and this is the key to it all.

The summer passes. I am trying to make the beach my home again.

The holidays roll toward us. We've had no Christmas for several years and this must be a beauty. There are various special treasures not usable in this new location. But I get stuck trying to wrap a huge round metal war gong brought from the Philippines on one of our freighter trips. A sharp jerk of frustration at unwieldy paper, a back gone like wildfire into deep spasm from buttocks to nape of neck, and I am frozen into pain again. Christmas — like the gong — hollow. The old routine of hospitalization, rest, hot packs, exercises, and whirlpool baths does nothing. I limp back to work and interview with my feet up in a lawn chaise. By June pain has dulled me so I can no longer remove myself and place my wisdom into the hands of my clients. I have no skills anymore. I resign. When all my clients are finally settled in with other workers, I leave, bearing my paraphernalia of plants, pictures, books, and dictating machine, and drive home with sinking heart which cries out, "I'm old!" Literally for the first time, I am looking at myself as an old woman of seventy-eight.

What's old? I look starkly into the long mirror and do not care for what I see until my ridiculous gremlins begin to giggle and I laugh, too, and my figure straightens and my face brightens. Not so bad. Okay! Old? Okay! So what next?

Very much bed-bound, except when I get my oversimplified meals, I begin reading on old age and discover lots of government and private concern and psychological and psychiatric theory. None of it I want! I want old age from the horse's mouth, to see what it is that I am coming to.

I begin my own book. There are fleeting times when I am so absorbed in a new idea that pours via nerve impulses, via my finger, via ink, onto a page, that my spasm seems to ease. So what's that about? Some damned psychosomatic activity that plays body against mind and mind against body but lets me occasionally feel a touch of the natural morphine that I would use were I an unselfconscious animal. Any animal.

As for the acute spasms, they were tossed from one doctor's hands to another. "You have to learn to live with it" — until I was directed to the Boston Pain Unit with its holistic approach.* This included every imaginable kind of therapy — relaxation techniques, meditation, psychiatric interviews, family interviews, biofeedback, on and on, at first very traumatic for any little princess. And the time comes, when in one great burst of determination, I mentally disinter Mother, visualize her in front of me, and kill her openly with ugly, ugly words before the rest of the psychomotor therapy group. I am free. When I leave I have learned that my "preciousness" was still active, how my superiority could make a wrong judgment, why it was so hard to stop being a social worker and become an ordinary patient; my crawl down the ladder toward simplicity was a tormented one. My anger had been very cleverly and deeply hidden. And infantile rage had so tightened a permanently damaged back there could be no relaxation of the whole muscular system without a kind of fundamental cleansing.

As a bonus, where I've been smoking two to three packs of cigarettes a day, on the morning after my symbolic destruction of the evil side of the relationship between Mother and me, I look at my cigarette, lay it aside, and this is my last one. Heretofore I had been totally unable to break the habit.

In the spring I go to the Insight Meditation Retreat at Barre, Massachusetts. Daringly, free from invalidism, I drive through miles of rain into an unknown area. Two weeks. Constant silence. Waking gong at four-thirty in the morning. All seated on mats in silence, wrapped in blankets in the great meditation hall by five. No speech whatever unless there is a meeting with a leader and oh, how lovely to be among such nice-looking people and not have to make any conversation whatever. Food vegetarian and extremely light. Each one of us with our daily

---

* For a detailed description of my experiences in the Boston Pain Unit (now the Massachusetts Rehabilitation Hospital), see *There's a Dance in the Old Dame Yet.*

chore. Sleep, after a supper of apple, nuts, and clear vegetable broth, is on a piece of foam rubber on the floor. And within that ambience I learn to withdraw my beehive of a mind back to some inner stillness that let me know, even if briefly, the utter peace of directed inaction.

July again — my eightieth birthday — and my book, *Bay View — A Summer Portrait,* is off the press. I can feel the family feeling me differently. A joyous summer. One drawback. Why do the gods punish? Who and when? My right eye had long since been struck down by macular degeneration with only some peripheral vision left. The other, I was told in June, was degenerating fast. No more driving. But not until I finish the first draft of my book on old age do I return to the Meditation Retreat and look directly into the eye of blindness where I could deal with sight loss and depression. Instead I learn that there could be challenge and whimsy and a stimulant to my untapped resources.

I have a choice of tremendous import that could lead me into the darkest corner of my being — a black hole where devils live — or accept, depressed, my hopeless incurable eye damage, never to see anything clearly again. With a certain macabre sense of humor, I choose the dance of life.

Feeling I am growing bigger inside all the time, and that a curious power is increasing in me, I start revision on the now accepted book under a special editor who urges that it be changed from essays to an autobiographical account of the past five years. Two revisions are done in five crazy months. Circumstances extremely difficult. I don't question whether I have the guts; it is where to find them. Seeing only dimly, using huge magnifying glasses, writing double- or triple-space with an extremely black pen in half-inch letters, driven by some force I do not understand, resting every hour with an aching back on the heating pad, a pillow under my knees, eyes closed in full palming relaxation, I am soon able to rise and get going again. Work has to be in the night hours, too — often one to four or two to five A.M., after I've had some sleep. Finally, all work done, last copy in. Nothing more until the copyedited book comes back.

My mind and I go empty for two months; I look at nothing. When in August the copyedited manuscript comes back to me for approval, I am puzzled. What relative can and will read it aloud to me and not be shocked! I glance at those strange pages. Then I touch them with a timid forefinger. Then I look. Ho! I can read in a bright light. The disintegrating eye has cleared for focusing. Miracle? Reward? Out of the summer's fallow soil the dragon's teeth have sprung up as warriors. Can I now look at our marriage, any marriage, without blinders?

I started this book.

PART TWO

They love dancing well that dance barefoot upon thorns.

— Thomas Fuller, *Gnomologia* (1732)

CHAPTER 22

Winter and the Dance Are Good

Now CAME a good winter in spite of my back pain, poor eyes, and bad circulation in the leg I had damaged aboard *Zuleika Dobson*. A drive to work on the new book was intense. For I must find out what love was and how it endured in that impossible situation of Man and Woman living too close together. In October I bought a new car and was independent again. Feeling gay, I acquired a vanity plate, "OVER 80." Why not shout it out? And this meant no more dependency on others for short errands. In my limited driving, no one ever tailgated me, no truck kept roaring its motor behind me. I was building up my body again by exercises and long walks, also trying to keep the improvement in the eyesight of my left eye by exercising it according to the Bates method. I played some bridge with large-print cards. I gave a couple of small cocktail parties. I could be with people comfortably and enjoy it.

The galley proofs of my previous book came. They had to be read by someone else, however. In December the director of the Atlantic Monthly Press, which had bought the book, called and said they wanted to change my title of "A Late Lark." It would be "There's a Dance in the Old Dame Yet," and they wanted me to like it. It would have more appeal on the bookshelves.

"What!" I said. I almost felt the hair rising on my head.

"Yes, you remember Don Marquis and his book on archy and mehitabel."

"I never read it that I know of."

He tried to explain. It didn't help. Was I an alley cat singing to the moon?

"Get a copy. Then you'll see."

I drove to the library and they had the slim old volume. Swiftly, at home again, I read it through. I saw that archy was a philosophical cockroach who wrote on a newspaperman's typewriter but was unable to use the shift key (hence all those lower-case letters). His best friend was mehitabel, the alley cat, who got into all kinds of disasters but became her pert self again after each sally, saying, "wotthehell wotthehell there's a dance in the old dame yet toujours gai toujours gai."

The humor of it all suddenly struck me. In my heart maybe I was an alley cat, a stray, and delight suddenly shook me. I got the director just as he was leaving the office and said, "Okay," then I sat and thought for a while. Then I poured myself a drink and at once started an epistle to him that expressed still confused feelings. It was written in the style of archy, *vers libre,* lower-case, and all. I give this just as I wrote it rapidly.

dear sir editor

though i am always a lady
and an aristocrat
i have never traveled
in intellectual circles
and so did not meet
your archy and mehitabel
now in my reincarnation
transmigration and
transmogrification

so admirably
maneuvered by you
i find myself joyfully astray
i take to alley cat existence
without paws or pain
liberty to dance is all i ask
and singing to the moon
what are late larks
but to snatch and eat
twitter and all
i always suspected
i had zest for life
and the gay encounter
on whory nights
but it took your
hind fore and insight
to point out to me
my true fishhead
dash loving self
however comma
please put this on my
garbage scow marker
when bad reviews have
finished off my ninth life
quotation mark
spin mehitabel spin
you had a romantic past
and you re gonna cash in dancing
when you are croaked at last
unquotation mark
wotthehell wotthehell

from that old dame mehitabel
toujours gai kid

p s one final gentle hopeful meow
isn t your first name tom
interrogation mark

p p s i have dictated
this epistle to archy
who mentioned that
he and his pals
have often partaken
of your fine hospitality period
happily exclamation mark

A reply came back from the director saying, in effect, "You've made my day. It was going to be a tough one." And from then on all formality ceased, and that sympathetic flow between editor and writer began.

Christmas was a fine one. We gathered and my presents to the descendants were most of my remaining pieces of sterling and some rare old books, either written by my great-grand-father, a scholarly, transcendental Unitarian minister, or ones even older, running back to 1500, that I inherited from his library. My grandchildren were to think of them as treasures, I told them, and we laughed at the difficulty they had in figuring out the Roman-numeral dates.

Excitement grew within me as well as at the Atlantic. Very favorable response was coming from the galleys that had been sent out. The book was now being printed and bound.

Almost at once in my writing came back the memory of that wink of mine at the marriage rites. Why? So I mentally titled my new book "The Wedding Wink." In April real excitement began. There was a letter from the publicity department giving the various local TV appearances I was to make, also one in-terview to be bounced off Telstar to Washington and to be broadcast on National Public Radio, live. What would it be like to be talking into a mike to an unseen audience? And what would I wear? And could I do it adequately, I who had never appeared in public like that before? I had two voice lessons to get away from the guttural sounds of the elderly and to enunciate and project. I practiced hard. I bought several new dresses by catalog.

Knowing nothing of TV except what appeared on the screen and knowing no one who had ever been on TV, I heard of a woman who specialized in helping ignoramuses through their novitiate on the tube. I called her and she came. Most capable and smart and affable. She would tell me what to wear, she said, would make me up, would instruct me, come and get me, stay with me, giving suggestions if necessary, and get me home safely. With my limitations of leg, back, eyes, and mentality, it sounded lovely. Cost? She looked through the schedule. $1,000. I declined with thanks.

Also, in April my right eye, the one that had only peripheral vision, went suddenly sightless. It was a hemorrhage, the doctor said, that would clear up. I found I tended to bump into things on my left side, and had difficulty in, for instance, figuring out how full to fill my coffee cup, and often pouring half outside.

One afternoon about five o'clock, Channel 5 called me to see if I would appear that night live on the program they carried. This was not a scheduled appearance. It would be my first.

"*Two* A.M.?" I asked incredulously. They would send a limousine for me, one they used regularly. I would be perfectly safe and well taken care of, as the driver would stay with me in the studio and get me home again.

The old lady who wouldn't be old — hadn't been out that late in decades — crazy business. But no one I knew would be up that late and see my fumbling and uncertainty. And what fun, adventure — wotthehell. I had only a moment of hesitation.

"Yes," I said.

"The driver will be there at twelve-thirty, and you'll be on in the two o'clock hour."

At twelve-thirty I was helped into a limousine a mile long. In the back where I sat with my feet up, the cushions were so deep and the windows so far forward that I was sitting in a safe, soft nest. And in a moment the chauffeur slid back the glass window and said, "There's a bar and a television there if you want to use them." I found that this North Shore Hollywood Limousine Service often drove couples to New York. I could well imagine what might go on in that softly cushioned little room, traveling along at a steady speed.

At the studio I was indeed taken care of. I gathered that I was a filler-in for somebody, for the emcee had not yet read my book, though he was carrying it under his arm as he spoke to me. In the large room a man sat silent in one corner. I sat in another with the chauffeur near me, and two other small groups. Twenty minutes each we were to have. The lone man came first. He turned out to be Alan Dershowitz, the lawyer, speaking on his controversial new book. One could watch from the large TV screen in the corner of the room. Then came a juggler, whose friends watched intently, then my turn. The interviewer read excerpts from the blurb on the book cover and then seemed stuck, but somehow we got going. I have no idea what I said or how. Then it was over. Twenty minutes of three. I lay down in the back seat all the way home, spent yet exhilarated . . . into bed at three-thirty A.M. So why not? But there were a couple of calls next day. I had not realized that anyone who knew me would be watching at that time of night. Poor sleepless ones.

Subsequent prepublication interviews went more easily, and they had good interviewers who were sympathetic with the book's message.

Now, in May, the book was on the shelves, and letters and telephone calls began to come in. Also requests of me to speak before an audience. And there I found that I had a fine store of adrenaline that was drawn out by a live audience like magic, for my mind seemed to dance.

About the time that *There's a Dance in the Old Dame Yet* first glared from bookstore shelves, I spoke publicly. It was at an authors' breakfast, where four of us sat at a long table with our names in large print before us, and there was a podium, I saw with dismay. The audience, after coffee and Danish pastries at round tables, moved to sit in rows before us. Miserably, I saw that the director of the Atlantic Monthly Press was among the listeners. When I stood, holding on tight at first, I talked about aging and the giving of birth to a book when so elderly, and about the new title. And my mehitabel-like *vers libre* to Mr. Brady, the director, at the change in title. (Was I teasing him?) And I spoke of the funny feeling it gave me to be standing there. For the book's real work and the emotional investment in it were many months behind me and I was reinvolved in new writing. And, I added, the only thing my heart said to me was, "Lawk-a-mercy on me, this be none of I!" And I quoted that wonderful nursery rhyme:

> There was an old woman, as I've heard tell,
> She went to market her eggs for to sell.
> She went to market, as I've heard say
> And she fell asleep on the King's highway.
>
> There came by a peddler whose name was Stout
> He cut her petticoats round about.
> He cut her petticoats up to her knees,
> Which made the old woman to shiver and sneeze.
>
> When this little woman did first awake
> She began to shiver and she began to shake
> She began to shake and she began to cry
> "Lawk-a-mercy on me, this be none of I!

But if it be I, as I hope it be,
I've got a little dog at home that sure knows me,
And if it be I he will wag his tail
And if it be not I, he will surely bark and wail."

So home went the old woman, all in the dark —
Then up got her dog and he began to bark,
He began to bark and she began to cry,
"Lawk-a-mercy on me, this be none of I!"

And I meant it.

There was a larger audience when I appeared before the Sociology Department at Brandeis University. The students were studying gerontology at that point. Older people were there too. My chair was not what I had requested. It was a straight-backed one. So, when I was introduced, I stood with one hand on the table to steady myself and started off. As discomfort seized me, I slid off my pumps and perched cross-legged in my pants suit — my most comfortable position — on the table top, and I talked about old age and all the naughty little things one can do to give it life and humor. Here I elaborated on what was in the book. There was a lot of laughter, and when I told them of smoking pot to ease pain before sleep and how I had obtained the pot through a granddaughter, there were shouts of amusement.

Another time, with a still larger audience of social workers and other therapists, I stood before a podium with a mike on it, and as I gestured I kept knocking off the soft covering of the mike and I'd stoop to pick it up with an amused gesture of despair. One of my great-grandmothers had been a quite noted actress, and I realized I had inherited some of her dramatic quality that was just now coming out.

The telephone became exciting, the mail became exciting. I hired a secretary one morning a week and dictated responses. People came to call; some of them were pleasurable and some tended to go into their own problems. I had to close the door on that.

The only time I felt a faint regret at having turned my $1,000 guide down was when I was interviewed on National Public Radio's "All Things Considered." A taxi was sent out to Lincoln for me and I was driven to station WGBH in Boston, to be met at the door of the huge building as requested. The girl who met me — call her Joan — said that my interview would be between Boston and Washington via Telstar and that it would be in a small soundproof room but that the way into it was through an interviewing studio which was momentarily being used for broadcasting. She would have to take me through the control room. Down one passage, another, my head down to watch for bits of boobytraps like thresholds or steps up or down. I could not focus on how we went. She put her fingers to her lips as we opened a door. I had a sense of a large room, a lot of switchboards or controls or computers and a lot of men silent before them. We slipped quietly through, and Joan opened another door and I found myself seated by a table in a small, inner, windowless room. There was a telephone on the table. Telstar. What fun. I waited with anxiety rising. Joan was in and out of the control room and on another telephone and finally said the Telstar was out of place or that we were out of place and they were putting a straight call through from city to city. A moment of disappointment. It had been the nearest I would ever get to heaven, even though it was only through my voice.

Soon Joan said, "Pick up the receiver. You're connected now." And she went out and closed me in alone. I heard a friendly sounding voice. Washington and I had a moment of chat and then "You're on now." The interview began, question and answer, and I had a vague feeling that all over the country I was being heard. I, Harriet, the timid little girl, the old woman. I guess the interview went all right, but I never knew afterward what I said. When it was over, with the repeat of the announcement of my name and of the book, the connection was broken off. I hung up and waited for Joan to appear. Five minutes? Ten minutes? I didn't dare go back through the control room. Finally I opened the only other door and entered an empty studio with, I think, two chairs on a dais. I walked through another door, I walked down a corridor, I walked up another one. I felt myself in a rabbit warren, no one in sight, no open doors. All I wanted was the ladies' room and the street door where a taxi would be waiting to take me home. I could have killed Joan for deserting me. For I was lost, utterly, blindly lost, able only to watch my footsteps.

Finally I hit on a cubbyhole with a small switchboard. Three women were there chatting and laughing. I said there was supposed to be a taxi waiting for me. Did they know if it had come and where, please, was the ladies' room? Why the hell didn't I tell them I was almost blind? No, they didn't know anything about any taxi and the ladies' room was down "that way." I couldn't find it. More wandering. More trying to read labels on doors, more trying to find my way out, out of that maze.

At last — a wider corridor, a glimpse of daylight at the end, and hope. It was the entrance hall with its glass doors. I went through them and drew a big breath of freedom. There was a row of taxis. Again, watching my footwork, I asked each of the drivers if he was for Mrs. Robey. The last one in line, waiting somewhat out of the way, was mine. The driver started from a half sleep, and jerked to alertness as I opened the rear door, got myself in, and curled up on the seat. Home at last, my own front door and my warm bathroom that waited within.

After that experience I made it clear, very, very clear, what my limitations were — back, balance, vision, leg circulation — and that I must be protected. I was. My escort either came and got me or was waiting at each station and carried my folding

146

lawn chair, my back cushion, my folding "gout" stool, and I carried my cane and pocketbook.

I never did see myself afterward in repeats of interviews. I never tried nor wanted to. And I never did wear makeup and no one ever suggested it.

CHAPTER 23

The Eye and the Winter Are Bad

Y UNSEEING EYE was getting painful, but at each visit the eye doctor suggested waiting a little longer. It would clear up. It didn't. In mid-July I was sent to Dr. R, one of the best of the new fancy-gadgeted specialists.

Dr. R's waiting room was in perfect decorator taste with a large square of fine plants in the middle of the room and muted colors. It was all rather antiseptic. After preliminary tests, I was ushered into Dr. R'soffice. There I waited for some time. He appeared. He did the fluorescein dye test. He did the sonar test. And finally he came up with a statement that ran roughly as follows.

The hemorrhage was behind the eye and the pressure had torn the retina and displaced it. It required an operation which they could do with a fairly good chance of success. But why hadn't I come sooner? On the other hand, considering my age, and the length and discomfort of the operation, he advised against it. Why the hell didn't I tell him how much that eye hurt? Because I'd been trained not to complain of pain. Because I'm a cringing nitwit when it comes to male surgeons. Why didn't he ask? He rose from his swivel chair and dismissed me with the words, "When you go out past the reception desk, make an appointment for a year from now."

Going out, I walked straight past the desk, was driven home, telephoned his office, and told Dr. R's secretary that I would like to have that operation and to please schedule it. There was fear in me now.

The eye operation, four hours long, six days in the hospital, of no vital seriousness yet peculiarly devitalizing, came and went. The operation consisted of clearing out behind the eyeball, mending the retina, taking out all fluid from the orb, and replacing it with lighter-than-air gas.

Back in my room and as soon as I was able to sit up, I was put in an erect posture against the head of the bed, which was raised to its straight perpendicular position. I was to keep that position day and night for four days with my head down as low as I could on my chest so the back of my eye was toward the ceiling. In this way, the gas would push the retina up against the socket and it would begin to reattach itself. This was a fine new form of torture in view of my spine's pinching a nerve whenever I sat erect. After a few hours of desperation, during which anxiety and rage rose with the pain, I took a pillow, laid it against the rail beside me, put my forehead on it, my chin on a little firm pillow I had brought to help my back, and with my hands making an airhole, I had my head and eyes in a down position. That ought to do it. The nurse saw me and ordered me to sit up at once. I pointed out to her that this gave the same effect for the gas and was the only tolerable position. She scolded again, and then called for Doctor R. When he came in and reproached me, I explained to him the purpose of that position. He looked at me for a moment, and then remarked dryly, "Sometimes we learn from patients." The rest of the four days I curled up, on one side or the other. But I knew only inactive nausea and intense discomfort. Dr. R called my reactions the "anesthetic syndrome." Did he have any idea of the sensitivity and the symbolic meaning of a severely traumatized eye? Could he guess at the quivering of the psyche?

A visit to him two weeks later. The eye was doing fine. Three weeks later, still doing fine. I asked, "Why no light coming in?"

"Blood left over from the operation. We didn't get it all out."

Three more weeks. He wasn't there, but an associate saw me, did the fluorescein and sonar tests of two months before, and said that everything was broken down again — another rip in the retina, another detachment. He called in the third associate from another office. Another operation at once: I was given the hospital appointment before I left the office.

I have notes I wrote desperately after I got home. I quote a little from them.

> Christ! I'm so sick of this eye pain and this nausea. Here I'm in the middle of the push of trying to write out my marriage via "The Wedding Wink" . . . "Mumsy, Mumsy! I need you now" . . . Let the lion lie down with the lamb. Tell the body it doesn't need to fight that old battle any longer . . . Why does the picture of Mona Lisa come to my mind so vividly? She seems ugly, snide, sneering, superior, I-know-what-you-don't-know, female, who watches all her daughters' unconscious thoughts but stands aloof, uncaring. And why the hell did I wink at my wedding?

> Depressed, depressed, depressed . . . No vitality, no interest, no energy, no caring, only helplessness and confusion. My brain is turned off. Oh, dear God! What do I do till the life comes back? But the children come to see me tonight and I must be cheerful for them. Yes, the old can be frightened, too. Of what? Of themselves.

Weeks passed. But the habits of the elderly are very comforting and sustaining, provided they don't become inflexible. Few of us care for unpredictability. And they did sustain me. The only things one can't control are dreams, so — awake between four-thirty and six soon to greet the day — bath, breakfast in bed, and at my working chair by eight-thirty or nine, thinking, writing. Light lunch. I would nap, work again, go to bed very early. But linger in bed and do nothing? Too uncomfortable because of my body and my early training. And the days and weeks and months passed. Writing continued.

Several visits to Dr. R. But the December visit showed the eye had collapsed once more. "We won't try again. The chances of success are too small. Come see me in a year." He didn't look at my other eye.

So that was that. Nausea and pain continued to be my daily bread, and it was a heavy, heavy weight. I could only say to the young, "No Christmas party here this year. And please, no presents." Little gifts came to the door, and I felt guilty. A large box of fresh holly, magnificent in its berries, arrived from a friend in Oregon. I cut them up in little bunches, tied a red ribbon around each, and left them at the doorknobs of those who had done thoughtful things for me. But I could not see people, deep though the Christmas need of love and contact was. I had to lick my wounds like an animal in hiding, and I felt guilty about my closed and locked door. My breasts were dry, my Philemon's pitcher empty.

Since the muscles of both eyes synchronize, and since I'm animated when I talk, and study people's faces, any strain of looking or dealing with more than one person still left deep eye pain.

Fairly fatalistic about the dead eye now, I worried about the other. It was beginning to see things as thick and blurred. I called up my own eye doctor, who was about to have an eye operation himself and who referred me to a woman doctor. "You'll like her," he said. She was a joy, warm, friendly, interested in a very human way.

Dr. B put me through the usual visual tests. Quite quickly, she said, "Blink." I blinked. "No, you're not closing the live eye so that the tear ducts in the lower lid can clear your eyeball.

It's covered with secretion. You're looking through a film." But I couldn't blink fully. The dead eye still would not close. "Put in saline drops every hour, but blink as often as you can. Make yourself blink." She patted my knee. I came home feeling rich, and the eye did clear up to what vision it had.

After that, I settled down even more seriously to writing. My condominium was so well insulated that I heard no sound of the neighbors, only the motors of the snowplow or blower, or the garbage truck, or a starting car — *if* I listened. And I didn't. I could hear the sleet on the double windowpane, but no draft penetrated, and I saw the trees waving. The snow was a luminous whiteness and isolated me even more securely. My children, if they came, brought in firewood so we could sit before the hearth. Mentally, I was remote and engrossed.

When I moved after Alec died, I made a den for myself of an extra bedroom and had three sides lined with bookshelves to hold all the leather classics I had inherited and other acquired favorites, including one shelf of books highly recommended in reviews that enlarged my current thinking. Most of these I never could read.

As an adolescent reading the nineteenth-century classics — Dickens, Hardy, Melville, Trollope, and my favorite for quieting tension, Jane Austen — I had imagined myself sometimes in a library lined with leatherbound books and with red leather-covered armchairs. With extra money from the sale of our old house, I blew myself to a dark red leather couch and an armchair and footstool of the same leather, and a black leather-topped desk with a file drawer among the others. The treasures from our freighter trips — always something old, mostly excavated, used and loved by people once, all with beauty of line, and everything with special feelings for me — were on alternate shelves in that room. And in my armchair before the wide window I would work, my dictating machine on a little table on the right, extra files of working material on a table on my left, the reference books within reach to the right of the dictating machine. To this spot I would go with anticipation, my mind holding in waiting the scene I had been working on the day before or in the early morning hours. When pain of back and eyes intruded, I rode my stationary bicycle or lay on my bed again to breathe deeply and let my muscles go as I palmed my eyes. Meditation was now useless. I could not still my mind. My working hours were between nine and twelve and two or three and five, usually with the telephone turned off. Everything in the house had to be neat and in order before I committed myself to that sanctuary.

Never during the two years of work did I allow myself to stay in bed, though I had breakfast there. Even in the evenings random thoughts might keep coming and end up on scraps of paper to be filed later under subjects. And the file boxes held titles such as anger, early marriages, recent marriages, divorce, sex and its variations, philosophy, religion and death, children, drugs and other escapes, women and men.

Those were indeed lovely hours of isolated and creative thought, even if the content of my writing held memories more often painful and rueful than happy.

And always, both day and night, I was dressed attractively for myself.

Almost two years of dedication to a search. For what?

January, February, March. Desolation? No, deliberate isolation. I felt as if I saw nobody. Yet looking back at my calendar, I saw several people a week, my intimates, aside from children's visits. I drew on adrenaline for the three or four talks I gave and did well, exhausted, although exhilarated, afterward.

The word spread, and the more casual friends learned not to come without telephoning first. My intimates brought me things — a problem in a way, for how could I repay them? I had to learn that I need not feel guilty; they got pleasure out of doing it. That was why I had to brace up at visits. Caroline, my newly widowed sister-in-law, and I talked several times a week, and if I didn't call, she would check in on me by phone. She also came bringing some special little dish made for me or a leftover. Several times she took me shopping for things that were further afield. Allie, younger and all-giving, brought unusual foods from stores, a rare flat Syrian bread, a carton of noncommercial delicate macaroons. I went once or twice to her house. Fresh bran muffins, rich chicken soup were occasionally left at the door. Betty, a mental stimulant with her literary interests, came weekly with three new-laid eggs brought by a farm friend of hers, and they were as welcome in their consistency and subtle taste as were those of my early memory, when, a child, I had the daily job of gathering the eggs in the chicken house, sliding my hand lightly under feathers, softly stealing out a warm brown and speckled shape. These eggs were for my father's breakfast — vivid, because it was identical year in and year out; fresh-cooked oatmeal with our own thick cream, a perfectly shaped and cohesive egg on his buttered toast, fresh ground coffee, and the quietness and pleasure with which he consumed it before going to work.

Once, in my fifties, I had visited Dr. Helene Deutsch at her experimental farm in New Hampshire. At lunch she and Dr. Felix mentioned that the hen house needed to be cleaned out.

"I'll do it, I've nothing else to do"; but out there I looked at my best new sandals, yellow suede with toe thongs, and thought, "Oh, oh." I slid them off, and with hoe and shovel cleaned out the muck of hen-shit. Back at the house I asked where the hose was. Dr. Deutsch looked at my feet.

"You did it barefoot?"

"Yes, my sandals were new."

She stared at me a moment and shook her head incredulously. Then she laughed. Did the high-born Europeans never muck themselves up? I felt both misunderstood and pleased that I could give her something to be surprised about.

CHAPTER 24

The Barn Revisited

I N JANUARY, the first half of the book — our marriage — was done, except for one key incident of my earliest childhood — so painful to recall, so influential on my life. An incident which even analysis could not bring to light.

It was around 1960, not long after Mother died, when the children were all settled in their own houses and Alec hadn't yet retired. I was laboring under the pain of the undiagnosed fractured vertebra, and this day had been one of spasm almost beyond tolerance. With my crazy-making brace on, I got Alec's supper, and while he rinsed the dishes and setttled down to TV, I got back to bed where my sleeping pill *cum* blind exhaustion took me quickly to sleep.

I woke, stunned by some ultimate horror of dream with my back crazily and deeply arched, and with a hideous, strange taste in my mouth, throat, and nose that started me gagging and choking. I turned on the light, sat on the edge of the bed, and shook. Bewildered, I had to come back to reality even as my mind asked, "What? Why?"

I walked around the house, emptied the dishwasher — still faintly warm — and had milk and cookies, and finally the craziness in my mind and throat subsided. Then another rescuing sleeping pill.

The next night there came almost the same nightmare, as if some electrode had touched within the brain its area of taste and smell. This time I took up my notebook in desperate earnest and at the same time in wild curiosity. Slowly, slowly under my pen the heavy fog of a strange anguish rolled away — a little distance. But what I saw I had to write in the third person.

Little Harriet, almost five, her brother Brooks, two and a half, who was wheeled in the perambulator by Lucy, their nurse, took the usual post-nap stroll up the short hill to the grandparents' great house where Lucy enjoyed her tea with the maids at the kitchen table, and Brooks was admired as usual.

Harriet, bored, feeling happy and light and saucy and flirtatious to herself in her clean starched dress, looked first into the circular greenhouse where grew the great purple winter grapes, then she danced into the big stable moving from bright sunlight into the cool dimness of the barn. There were the horses in their stalls but she liked the one in the box stall best. She moved further in. Then hands grabbed her, rough, rough hands — her back forced violently backward — nothing more . . .

Her next memory was starting down the hill for home, Lucy hurrying, and Harriet holding tightly to the upright bar of the stroller — the only safe thing on earth, something real to make you real.

Now I was myself again writing in my notebook, for no more memory came and my pen said, "I'm almost touching some answer. Go on! Don't run away — it can't kill you. Go on, feel! Think! Don't be afraid." But nothing more did come, no clues, and I *was* afraid.

The next night the dream was a continuum. I was lying in a bed facing the door and standing at the foot of the bed were Mother and the doctor, and Mother's face was distorted with wild rage; a Medusa face as she looked at me and at the same time it seemed as if her hideousness blinded me. I had done something too dreadful to know. But what! Oh, Mother, Mother, you're not you.

And then I saw, as if written on the wall in great letters, the words, "They looked in the wrong place." It was like the warning *mene, mene, tekel, upharsin* — the warning of dire destruction for Belshazzar, who was killed the next day.

I could now — shortly after Mother's death and in an extraordinary return of the repressed under maddening pain — I could now guess what had happened, but never the exact details, not even to this day of writing. I suspect that at a certain point in the trauma I lapsed into unconsciousness.

But with what relief now did everything begin to fall into place. I could comprehend the wild raging distortion in Mother's face, it being obvious that some man had molested her daughter. I could see why I was allowed to sleep with her while Father was temporarily banished to the guest room and why I had the nightmare that made me rush out into the hall before my parents had gone to bed and Mother hurried up the stairs at my wails and I could only tell lies as to what was upsetting me, not knowing myself why. Or understand why perhaps I got the infected ear and had to have it regularly punctured until the eardrum drained and healed quietly, meanwhile finding a strange joy in the doctor's infliction of pain. Or why Mother and Father, barely five years after building their new house, on a piece of Grandmother's land, had gone out into a country farm town (an unheard-of event socially), a town that held a church and minister, an office with doctor, a general food store that had pickles in a great jar with scum on the top, and a bandstand that I never saw used — gone out at some inconvenience to start a new life of innocence for their children — a place where nightly dreams went on, for me of the train's cowcatcher grinding me up in pain and terror and spewing me out by the trackside in a kind of masochistic ecstasy.

And why I became so anorexic that Father, steeped in economy as he was those days, offered me a dollar a pound for every
one I gained; why I came to eat so often at Uncle Tom's house
where the food seemed delicious; why I always had a finger in
my mouth. (Mother remarked one day, "If saliva was a bright
blue color your face and hands would be a horrible sight" —
that seemed like another awful sin.) Why I still and to this day
tend to sleep with my hands covering my mouth, the pressure
having killed the nerves in two teeth. Why I never have been
able to hold a pin or paperclip or cigarette between my lips
unless my fingers are holding it. Why, why, why?

Why I was too frail to go away from home, plead though I
did for camp. Why when at last I persuaded them to allow me
to go to college, I gained twenty pounds by Christmas in spite
of having the 1918 influenza. Why I was so afraid of sex and
sexuality even beyond Mother's strictures and warnings. Why
I waited on her so sedulously and watched her face so carefully
that never, never, never would I see that look on it again. Why
I have been terrified all my life of anybody drunk, violent,
attacking, or pimply-faced.

Ever since have I searched for that gap in memory. Even this
writing can only bring up terror of a man's penis.

Why I needed to suffer and be in pain and be sick. No
snapshot from childhood ever shows me with anything but a
sad and solemn face. And I wore an iron brace for scoliosis and
swayed back, and braces on my teeth, and my hair was thin and
fine and long and straggly, but I grew belatedly into someone
Alec wanted to marry.

It was several years after the recall before I could mention
the "barn man" to Alec and then gradually to the children. I
can speak of it quite comfortably now. Such things do happen
to children. Such things do scar children. Such things do affect
one's relationship with a mother when no help comes from her
just when the hurt is at its greatest.

158

But when we played in the barn in Tewksbury — one of our favorites was tag, or hide and seek where we had built many tunnels in the full hayloft — Mother often walked down to see what we were up to and frequently asked if Roberts, the farmer, was ever "fresh" with us.

And finally I understood my compulsion to find situations where I could lose or I could master. I had to dare to dare. Somehow I must repeat that dark terror in that dark barn in an attempt to drive it out. Master or be mastered, repeated over and over.

And finally, too, I understood why Mother with her own primitive psyche could, on my wedding eve, make that symbolic gesture to kill any overt sexuality that I might have. This was a matriarchy, this family of mine, and sex was taboo.

But also why should she send me over to Uncle Tom? Did she have some totally unconscious sense that there might be something going on there? (Oh, that dreadful question when I reached home, "What did you and Uncle Tom do tonight?")

Or why Mother was severely polite with Alec (he never ceased to call them Mr. and Mrs. Stevens) as if she spotted early a certain sadism in him and grieved that here would be another trauma for me. Or was it just profound fear of sex?

CHAPTER 25

Up and Down with Eye and Book

$\mathscr{T}$HE RELIEF that came with the assurance within myself that the episode in the barn had really happened was like an inspiration, unpleasant though the details were. After getting that incident down in words, I could be done with it, and the first half of the book was finished. I sent it to the Atlantic Monthly Press. It was accepted at once, a contract sent and signed, and the director came out to see me. He asked if I would accept him as working editor. Would I!

A couple of weeks later he sent me a large postcard with a photograph of an old lady taking a camera shot of a gorgeously endowed nude young figure posing seductively. On the back he wrote, "Will the real Harriet Robey please stand up? You bet she will . . . ["The Wedding Wink"] is going to be one hell of a book . . ." That postcard was a sudden delight and joy and a wonderful symbol of my youth and old age. I asked him if we could use it as a frontispiece to the book. He laughed. "We'll see."

What next? While I had been reseeing our marriage, I had been looking simultaneously at the pain in all marriages. I drew from the reality of ours and others I had known in life and social work.

I wrote reams of philosophical ponder-notes. I knew that

most of what I said was in the press, on TV, in articles and endless books. And I found our married life was easy compared with many. No severe illnesses or accidents, no deaths, no pressures from the world outside our extended family. What was so bad about it? The marriage state itself — the bonding of two totally different types of personality? The battle of the sexes? A power struggle which started soon after or even during the honeymoon?

And sometimes I wondered why couples can't love and touch and caress each other and look into each other's eyes. Just once in a while. It's all right to get cleanly angry and have it over with and let the sun come out again, just as Alec and I did when we appealed to "Dr. Robey."

The best description I know of intradomicile control is in Trollope's *Barchester Towers*. Bishop Proudie, having achieved the bishopric of Barchester through a political fluke, yet remained a hen-pecked man even in that exalted position. Rebel though he would, *she* was the one who decided all major non-ecclesiastical isues of the diocese. The worm turned at last. Bishop Proudie and his conniving curate, Mr. Slope, won their victory by tactfully ousting Mrs. Proudie from a decisive conference. A proud and victorious and worshipful man was the timid bishop then.

After dinner he returned to his study where Mr. Slope soon found him, and there they had tea together and planned many things. For some few minutes the Bishop was really happy; but as the clock on the chimney piece warned him that the stilly hours of night were drawing on, as he looked at his chamber candlestick and knew that he must use it, his heart sank within him again. He was as a ghost, all whose power of wandering free through these upper regions ceases at cock-crow; or rather he was the opposite of the ghost, for till cock-crow he must again be a serf. And would that be all? Could a man trust himself to come down to breakfast a free man in the morning?

He was nearly an hour later than usual, when he betook himself to his rest. Rest! What rest? However, he took a couple of glasses of sherry, and mounted the stairs. Far be it from us to follow him thither. There are some things which no novelist, no historian, should attempt; some few scenes in life's drama which even no poet should dare to paint. Let that which passed between Dr. Proudie and his wife on this night be understood to be among them.

He came down the following morning a sad and thoughtful man. He was attenuated in appearance; one might almost say emaciated. I doubt whether his now grizzled locks had not palpably become more grey than on the preceding evening. At any rate he had aged materially. Years do not make a man old gradually and at an even pace. Look through the world and see if this is not so always, except in those rare cases in which the human being lives and dies without joys and without sorrows, like a vegetable. A man shall be possessed of florid youthful blooming health till, it matters not what age. Thirty — forty — fifty, then comes some nipping frost, some period of agony, that robs the fibres of the body of their succulence, and the hale and hearty man is counted among the old.

He came down and breakfasted alone . . .

Intolerance in marriage seemed to boil down to incompatibility — the physical and psychical differences in the nature of male and female, each with his and her "I, I, I." Then why so many divorces and remarriages? Why marry at all? Because of the Great Loneliness again, the aloneness, search as one will?

Perhaps it all came back to the old nature and nurture. Nature gave the male the different physique, different sex needs (a billion million spermatozoa to die without his awareness during his lifetime, all that DNA for naught); his need to control, master, and win. The pleasure in the excitement of anger. Nurture has taught him that Big Boys don't cry, and the rough and tough and tumble is encouraged by toys that he can use violently. His training to manhood has begun while he would still like to be tenderly cuddled. So, I thought, he has to deny acknowledgment of any tender feelings within himself, and the door is also closed to the subtler feelings of others.

The female's body is built for childbearing, nursing, and rearing. Her one ovum a month, wasted or not, affects her daily life, practically and psychologically. Even at my age I still think of my children in their mature pain in terms of a symbolic ache in my womb. A woman's feelings are near the surface, having to be sensitive to those dependent on her strength. We hate violence. And in our own childhood the goal of being a pretty, dainty, little princess is before our childish eyes. Look at almost any very small girl and you see instinctual flirtatiousness.

And the man wants his wife to be *his*, sexy for his needs, loving, beautiful, a mistress and a mother to him, a good cook and a wise parent to the offspring. He may refer to her as "the old woman" or "the missus" when with other men. And I've heard fathers address their wives directly as "Mother." His wife must never be emotional or create problems or say, "I'm too tired."

And she wants him a Sir Lancelot, a good breadwinner, a lover, a tender caring father, and a man who can understand her needs.

Impossible. So why marry? Two things: we're caught in the biological drive to mate and reproduce. The other, the need to belong, to be part of something. We survive either through those occasional warm moments of companionship and the wonderful whole close contact of flesh with flesh in bed, or there is a drawn and permanent battle. Or a couple can fight openly and then make love and make up.

At this point, I found myself writing the following.

Marriage. Putting it cynically but whimsically, boy meets girl — man meets maid. Love is blind. He sees her as pretty as a picture, cute as a bug, sweet as honey, gentle as a dove, mild as milk, pure as a lily, patient as a monument, more fun than a barrel of monkeys, and eager as a beaver for sex. And she's as good as his mother's apple pie. And hot as Tophet in bed.

He has neglected to study her mother.

She sees him as God's gift to woman, and they marry. She has swept him off his feet as clean as a new broom. But woman is a "sometime thing" and as the months and years pass with their pressures, anxieties, and frustrations of childbearing and rearing, and depending on her makeup, he may see her wet-dishrag-limp, pickle-sour, bedbug-crazy, goose-silly, wet-hen-mad, fox-sly, iceberg-cold, mare's-nest-messy, a mid-stream horse-changer, gadfly-biter, nail-tough, pancake-flat, owl-stupid, old-sow-mean, snake-subtle, vinegar-sour, dog-sick, high-horse-rider, hog-on-ice-slippery, applecart-upsetter, bean-spiller, wrong-tree-barker, fire-coal-heaper, dead-horse-flogger, crocodile-tear-weeper, doornail-dumb, ditch-water-dull, and cold as a witch's tit.

Why do I pick women here instead of men? Because I know them from years of social work and observation. I know us. Do I hate women or am I compassionate with their reactions because they can't stand the pain? Let us hope they become as comfortable as an old shoe in their old age — *if* they stay married.

I was spinning my wheels.

I thought, pondered, philosophized; but nothing made sense to me. Not since July had I been able to meditate or relax.

Obtaining a large poster of the Mona Lisa, I hung it on my study door, where from my chair I could look at it, and try to penetrate that face as I went in and out of the room. She had appeared to me in the fall at the hospital, enigmatic; she had seemed superior and in a way disapproving. Now I began to read other expressions into her, and gradually she grew very important to me as a theme.

I didn't feel the "poor me" syndrome now. The pain of other human beings rode me. I wallowed in the misery of divorce, crime, murder, all the worst side of humanity.

I felt so sorry for others who saw no path ahead. My own

misery would fade in time as the eye cleared. I could sit and wait it out. I looked up at the Mona Lisa; as she seemed to grow more friendly, I called her La Gioconda and then eventually La G. Her intent look followed me.

Searching and feeling more and more widely, I lived all the loneliness of Man, each male and female seeking or giving up in a search for something lasting and secure and loving and close and clean, almost never to be found. That latent loneliness in the human being without a companion in true relationship.

Somewhere or other along the months of failing vision, I had been taught the Bates exercises and the palming of my tired eyes — one hand rounded against each eye without pressure and the fingers of one folded across the other so light was utterly excluded. A very pleasant, restful feeling. Then while breathing softly and evenly, I learned to focus on some particular peaceful and well-loved spot — and in imagination watch quietly some little scene or action in slow motion. The particular spot I always went to at once was the beach. Here I might study a periwinkle, white-pointed or dark-rounded, or follow the seaweed waving back and forth with ripples of incoming tide as it turned from crisp light brown to deep greenish color; or follow a sailboat floating out of our harbor before a very light wind; or, a child again, peer under the crevices of our little granite pier to find shade-loving sea life, my eyes never completely still but almost totally relaxed. This was to me a form of meditation, and my eye tension and head rigidity always seemed to ease.

But one day in April, my palming gave me an unwelcome picture. And I could not keep my eyes floating long. My whole body these days was too tense, even to the gritting of teeth, a sore neck and chest muscles, and jumpy legs. Grief again. And anger. I could not imagine quietly. Even though I went down to the beach mentally, I could not find that peace. Instead, my imagination insisted on taking me to the tip of the point of the island where waves sucked in and out gently when the sea was calm. Here my inner eye saw only one object, a little white rowboat containing a sturdy little girl in a bright red jacket, rowing, rowing out to sea, rowing with determination and with the accuracy of a piston beat. Out and out, smaller and smaller, and yet still I could see the red jacket and the thrusting energy that carried the determined little figure away and out toward the iceberg part of the Atlantic, and I wanted to cry, "Too soon! Come back, come back."

"Stop it!" I said to myself, but I kept seeing her. Intimations of mortality? Or a death wish? For my dead eye was growing very uncomfortable. Or could it be a final farewell to childhood? Or maybe the vision meant something I couldn't grasp.

I visited my eye doctor. Glaucoma. Extremely high pressure. Too much scar tissue to create drainage. Eye must be removed at once. That was on a Thursday. On Sunday I entered the Eye and Ear Hospital for the third time. Looking back, I remember nothing, for I was on autopilot. I packed toilet articles, notebook, radio, and all the usual pretty little nightgowns and bed-jackets.

And I worried.

After the right eye was removed, my surgeon's parting shot, as he signed me out of the hospital was, "Make an appointment with Dr. J for a month from now, but there's so much scar tissue he may not be able to fit a prosthesis and we may have to do some reconstructive surgery."

I was angry. Why tell me now? Don't they ever understand the anxiety over eyes? A burden falls on someone whose eye is removed. The eye and the "I" are so closely intertwined. And with those painful severed muscles in the right eye socket, I did not want to move my remaining eye at all. It could fix on a page of writing, but it was difficult getting out of my chair and focusing on motion or doing other things, and seeing more than one person at a time was even worse.

Looking at La G, I alternated between seeing the good and bad in woman. Was I injecting myself into her or her into me? I knew the awful sadistic things I had written out in my diaries, my agony columns, scribblings in earlier periods of pain. I knew that recently I had thought almost exclusively about pain.

Alternately, way underneath, I saw myself as noble, a good wife, self-sacrificing and giving, or I saw myself as one of the worst. Yet didn't I devalue other women who seemed weak and passive compared with me and who must be scorned or helped?

More and more I looked at the picture of La G, and could get a glint of compassion along with her firm directness. Who was she? What was she saying?

She's a beautiful, intellectual, volatile, divine, demonic woman. Conventional and complex, standing supremely civilized against the primordial background, and her psyche reaches back to the most primitive chaos; a great formal simplicity against time-lessness of infinite space and back to the beginning of time.

La Gioconda knows only a great creative maternal force — to produce and with it to nurture with caring. The sadness is that the nurturant seed may go wrong, wither and die. She knows all the suffering that man and nature have made. The coolness in her eyes is of one who has seen it all, but there is also an expression of one not able to save and who has learned to look squarely at life with self-containment when one is not able to counteract the wrong choices and the willfulness of man's mind.

The little half smile is of amusement? Pleasure? Love? She knows all the overwhelming unstoppable progression of seed with ovum, of life, birth, and death. She stands inevitably for self-knowledge of the past and of one's self. Could I draw from her a bit of immortality? Become a drop in that river that goes on forever? She is so unthreatened. When I was afraid of those eyes and that face and that smile I could not see her whole. Then I wondered: is she part of the timeless background of infinite space? Her hands were so calm and relaxed as if accepting fate. Is she demoniac in her knowledge of all evil?

No, she has forgiven herself. She has lost the word *evil*.

At the end of April, I wrote in my personal notebook,

> Recovering. Job's anger is mine now, and his wife's anger is unforgiving. So let's look at it. Whatever is wrong with me, it's blocking my writing. Apathy! Fury at doctors for a whole year now. I can't read surgeons and they can't read me. It's happened all the way through my medical history. All right, I'm angry, angry, angry, and frustrated. Is there some denial I arouse in doctors? Or is it my own inability to complain? All right, wash your hands of all doctors (not my sons) and get down to work.

Months before, I had committed myself to speak at a Unitarian church that yearly held a women's Sunday. It was to be May 1, May Day, two weeks after I left the hospital. Public exposure in an eye patch. To stand and give the sermon. The committee had heard about the operation and gave me an out. Hell, I'd go, and drink it neat. I prepared nothing — wait and see what was the mood and focus of the congregation and what preceded me. I had to fight my reluctance.

I could see little but the great starkly pristine church and the congregation, mostly female. A half hour passed as I sat up there with two other women who spoke. From the floor, to a piano, "I Am Woman," was sung, also several unrecognized hymns. Then I was introduced with some remarks about "the Dance" and a reference to my being a "wise" woman, the woman I had once dreamed to be.

Then I stood. The pulpit was a simple brown wooden structure with a shelf hidden in the back that held a glass of water, two books (Bible and prayer book?), and a flashlight. I began with my spiritual and intellectual great-grandfather, the transcendental Unitarian minister, who kept diaries and whose first sermons after he graduated from Harvard Divinity School in 1835 I referred to. His new message was not well received there in Bangor, Maine, where he had been sent as a *locum tenens*. There were three sermons every Sunday that he had to give. Each week there were fewer and fewer in the congregation. And he wrote, "What do they want from me, anyhow?" Now I expressed my gratitude for being allowed to speak from the pulpit of a Unitarian church.

After that, I went on "sermonizing" for twenty minutes or more. I have no idea what I said, except for the closing words, which came to me suddenly. "Walk tall, my daughters, and with generosity."

There was great and prolonged applause. So my adrenaline was still available, and I was taken home after coffee, warm and enriched, and glad that there was some dance in me yet.

CHAPTER 26

Lama

WHILE I was still unconscious from the removal of my eye, a white prosthesis was inserted in the socket, and when I first looked at myself in the mirror here was this white eyeball staring at me. I kept it covered. A month later, the real prosthesis was made. It was fascinating to watch the expert molding it to the scarred eye socket and then painting it in exact imitation of my other eye even to the blood vessels in the white, the yellow brown flecks dotted into the hazel background. (Ah, memory. My first beau had said my eyes were "flecked with gold.") The "artisan" offered me the little white cup-shaped oval, saying with a smile, "You might like it as a souvenir." He put it in an envelope.

Home from his office, I studied it. Oh, throw it away. No! I knew on impulse.

On a Chinese curio whatnot, taking up several bookshelves, sat, among other Oriental treasures inherited from grandparents and great-grandparents, a white stone Chinese kneeling figure about six inches high and delicately carved. His robes gave a quality of richness in their simplicity and line as they were draped about him. His hands were folded upon his lap as if they once held something in them. The fingers were exquisitely carved, and both thumbs were missing, either broken off or deliberately absent. His hat was a high one, rather like a biretta without its point, his face had wrinkles of humor around the eyes, and the mouth had a slight smile. There was good humor in that face and definite amusement.

Three years before, when I had been at the Insight Meditation Retreat for two weeks, there occurred an important event. The highest lama in Tibet was to visit this place among others on his tour of retreats in the United States. We were all sitting in our rows on our mats in the great hall, mostly cross-legged, as we meditated. We knew of the high priest's coming. He was borne in on a raised rectangular litter without roof, sitting in a chair in his rich robes. His bearers were all monks in saffron. The litter having been set down on the dais before us, we lined up on one side, some hundred and fifty of us, to receive his blessing. He was very important indeed, for he had been the one who had gone to China to plead that the Chinese should not invade Tibet. When he found his errand was fruitless, he returned to tell the Dalai Lama to get out of Tibet and to go down to the plains.

So there the holiest of holies sat and with an outstretched hand containing either a wand or a tassel-tipped light stick, I saw him lightly touch the shoulder of each of us yogi, or meditators, as we bowed before him. Then each passed by and a monk laid over his or her head, again bowed, a fine red silk cord, symbol of having received the blessing from on high.

When my turn came, I approached with slightly bowed head, was touched on the shoulder, and then stood and looked straight into his face. His eyes came from a distance, were startled, and then stared into mine. It was suddenly reminiscent of the wedding wink. What impulse it was I do not know, but I needed to look into those eyes to see if something could be communicated between us. One, two, three seconds, then I bowed my head, stepped aside, and had the red cord put around my neck. I walked across the floor and reached the group of those already blessed and now looking on. Someone hugged me — I think it was one of the staff. I wondered why.

Back home again with that fine red cord, I wondered what the hell to do with it. Then the idea came. I wound it round and round the neck of my little Chinese figure and arranged it to hang in graceful loops and there it sat.

Now I was sitting with my little white inverted cup and I impulsively moved and placed it on the hands of my Chinese priest. It fitted the space perfectly. "Ha," I thought, "symbols again. A begging bowl." And then I took a high-power magnifying glass and studied his face more closely. I couldn't believe it. The right eye was slightly opened and I could see the eyeball. The left eye was closed. In a wink?

CHAPTER 27

College Revisited

*L*A G BECAME more and more absorbing to me. Dramatic in comparison with the gentle mother of the Pietà beside it, who was a sorrowing if conflicted woman, mild and accepting, La G was life itself. As weeks passed, there came into my vision as I studied her periodically, a feeling of greatness, sadness, inevitability, tenderness, repetition through eternity, and a feeling of continuity. She seemed dispassionate, as if she had known too much too long, yet I could see the hint of humor, the twinkle of the eye, the lift of the mouth. I saw that she had been limned with such subtlety that one could read into her almost any expression one wished. So what was she saying to me and how was I interpreting her?

Studying her primordial background, against which and from which comes the figure in its sophisticated velvet dress, I searched for clues and found myself going back to college days when I was a premedical student. I sat at a table in the biology lab. It was a long table that held four seats on each side in which sat eight young women. The sun shone intensely down on us. And there was placed in front of each of us a large, wet, stinking dead cat. The smell of formaldehyde was overwhelming. We had our dissecting cases open, and the first cut was a challenge that held our fear. We were learning about the brain and the body: physiology, not psychology. We learned about the ascent of Man. We "pithed" a frog, which was worse than the first cut on the cat, since the frog was alive. A fresh ox heart was brought in and by some mechanical means it was made to beat, and we could observe its functions. A body was extraordinary in its complexities.

So little else did I get from college that I can now remember. Chemistry was a nightmare. All I have left is H_2O and H_2SO_4, and a few of the symbols for minerals. Always in that laboratory was the smell of rotten eggs, hydrogen sulfide. Always in the chemistry classroom were symbols on the board, and I can't think in symbols, I think from the gut. From physics I remember only the leap of metal filings toward a magnet and the long-drawn-out ring of the tuning fork. Einstein was completely beyond my comprehension. And philosophy, economics, politics, all had no interest whatever, no reality in my mental isolation. Looking still further back, I find all that's left from three years of high-school Greek, in which I went painfully through the *Anabasis,* the *Iliad,* and the *Odyssey,* is a small part of the alphabet and one meaningful thing, *gnothi seauton* (know thyself), the dictum of the Oracle at Delphi.

No, what *did* live was the long, long march in the ascent of Man. The most important thing to me was that out of the sea Man evolved over billions of years. In the fetus at a certain stage were gills, rudiments of the past, or the useless appendix and tonsils. I knew where I came from. Out of the salt sea.

By the time I finished college, I realized I was a mental runt, and that further pursual of medicine was hopeless. It was even a case of whether I would graduate. I had never in my college life gotten a grade above an 80, a single 80 in four years. The night before Commencement, there was a meeting of the authorities as to whether I and another girl — I never knew which one — would be allowed to graduate. It was early evening when I was informed that I would get my degree.

Mother and Father had come from Boston for my graduation. And that evening we were to dine with a rich cousin of Father's before taking the midnight train home.

My graduation dress, picked by Mother — I can see it so clearly because I loved it — was of heavy white linen with two-inch-wide inserts of handmade Belgian lace set in here and there, quite original and pure-looking compared with the fussier ones of my classmates. I remember nothing of graduation or what succeeded until we arrived at the Boltons' for dinner and found it was a formal dinner party at a house on Philadelphia's Main Line. There was a great party being given for the unmarried twenty-five-year-old daughter of the house. A most festive affair, on a huge estate.

I shrank and shriveled as I saw that the men were in tuxedos, the women in long, beautiful, flowing evening dresses — some ten couples, and an entertainment of a treasure hunt carefully planned and planted on the extensive grounds, the clues hidden here and there in the shrubbery and woods, and Japanese lanterns hung among the trees. Lots were drawn for partners and I looked dubiously at mine, a very sophisticated-looking older man. Like the others we started off together into the darkness and almost immediately my escort disappeared. I suspected that rather than rejection of me there must be some one girl he was interested in, but I felt more and more lonely and more and more lost. I wandered. I could hear shouts and laughter here and there in the distance, and I meandered in the dark, eerie in the occasional red lantern glow, the lights of the house in the distance. I, just graduated from Bryn Mawr, was a child in a child's dress, treated as a child, feeling like a child, unwanted.

I finally found myself beside a huge swimming pool. Until my fourth year of college I had been allowed no active sports because of a heart murmur. But that was gone my senior year and I played forward on our class water-polo team. Water was a familiar element from earliest childhood. And I stood beside that pool, looking down at its darkness, and I drew a great breath of air and leaped, landing with an enormous splash well out into the middle and sank to the bottom, exhaling slowly, until finally I could hold out no longer and I pushed myself up to the surface. Ah! There were yells and shouts, one man had his coat off about to jump in and rescue. Others came running from all directions. I was hauled out rather roughly, and led to the house and given beautiful underwear and my hair was rubbed dry by a maid and I emerged in one of the daughter's long and flowing evening dresses, the dubious heroine of the evening. A lot of apologies came my way.

We were chauffeur-driven into Broad Street station, I in my now dried and pressed clothes, and as Mother and I washed up in the Pullman's little triangular dressing room and were brushing our teeth, Mother said softly, "Did you do that on purpose?" She'd found me out again. Did I answer? I don't know. Father never said anything. He never did say anything.

There was no more mental growth in me until I plunged into psychoanalysis fifteen years later. There I took my first awed and awesome step into the unconscious, and my weight of depression lifted with the entering of that wide-open door of permission and acceptance, though many were the times I fell back into my slough as I struggled away from what I saw. This was my Pilgrim's Progress. I learned about the id, the ego, and the superego, a particularly unbalanced trio, as well as the Oedipal conflict.

In social work I studied theory and practice, and from my own clients and weekly case conferences with other workers, I translated what I had found out about myself into seeing all human beings going through what was essentially common to Man, albeit sometimes more strange or violent than I had conceived of. Strict self-control was part of social-work training, and I had to study myself further to eliminate any errors in treatment.

But I did learn to treat, and I learned the extremes to which the neurotic or psychotic mind could lead. What was bizarre and alien and vicious became the tragedy of lives in need of help. One single incident drove into me the connection between emotions and the brain. Our daughter, then aged eight, complained of abdominal pain one evening. It seemed to grow. I called Dr. Robey, who came to the house, took it seriously as a possible appendix, called in a surgeon friend who found the white blood count high. We took her to the hospital for an appendectomy. I stayed close to her and asked permission to go with her to the operating room until she was under anesthesia. Getting into a white coat, I stood by her head, telling her one of the fabulous stories of an oak tree in the forest covered with ivy behind which was a little door leading down to a magical place of toys. Miraculously, one could take out one's airplane and fly around the house, one could find or create a doll's house of wonderful delights. This story could be extended endlessly. I stood there, my voice holding her fascinated, while she was being prepped, and I ceased only when she became unconscious. I asked if I could stay and watch. Dr. Robey looked at the surgeon, who looked at me and nodded. I was given a cap and mask. When the appendix was reached it was intact.

"Shall we take it out while we're in here?"

"Why not?"

It was done. When she was back in her bed, I sat beside her, watching for the first stirrings. When they came, I continued the story, inventing more and more beautiful things and episodes. Dawn came on, and she dozed off to sleep. But I stayed with her until it was time to go to social-work class.

The first class that day was a visit to the Boston Psychopathic

Hospital, where we were to see what an EEG (electroenceph-alogram) was like. There were about ten of us. The instructor showed us charts of a normal brain wave and that of a psychotic; the first, a smooth but wiggly line with a few spikes, the other with sharp and far larger peaks, in very erratic order. We were asked who would like to be the subject. No one spoke. Finally, I said that I'd be the goat, and sat in the chair and had the disks stuck on my head, the wires attached, and the machine turned on. When we looked at the chart at the end, nobody spoke but all stared at it, then at me. It was almost identical to the chart of the schizophrenic. I could only say, "I've had no sleep for thirty-six hours. I was up all night with my child in surgery. I've had no breakfast."

What I saw was that my cool and quiet and tender involvement in her emotional fear, my watching the operation and having to make a decision, my determination to go normally to the nine o'clock class, were in total conflict with all the instincts of anxiety and fear of operations and excitement that called for action and some of the lower emotions. According to the tracing, I was temporarily schizophrenic.

More and more, as years passed, my curiosity about man's mind and psyche had grown. My scraps of notes had been constantly accumulating on the subject of the development of life. Suddenly the words *reproductive imperative* came to my mind. I saw why, in the individual, the fetus had already set aside in the second trimester all the genetic material in readiness for adolescence to give the signal. And that the family, that nuclear unit of all human species, had proved to be vital in the great biological urge.

I'd heard that if you put a single sexless amoeba at each end of a large tank of water, they will work toward each other. Was this the beginning of the fear of loneliness from separateness? And I had learned that in one special case if there is a threat to existence through drought to a large amoeba colony, the individuals will gather together in a kind of column, those at the top creating spores to survive the malignant conditions, while the lower ones die. Was that the beginning of cooperation and altruism? The climb up the ladder and out on its many branches was a familiar one. Each specimen, with its choice. Up the ladder where its choice became instinct, up the ladder in sea and land to insects to reptiles to birds to mammals. In one line, up and up to ape man, to the upright posture, the opposed thumb, the heft of a stone or stick, to fire, always in groups. Mate with the best. Pass on the finest seed. Make gods or higher powers to account for earthquakes, lightning, floods, pain and fear — what cannot be controlled without and within. So what?

I, the end product of all this evolution, could not write meaningfully. Writing out our marriage had been all done with total brain/pain, and my body, already uncomfortable enough, tensed and quivered again to all the dissonant discomforts of the past. The pleasures of our life together were lacking in richness. Was it anger and resentment that vibrated?

I could only sit and think and ponder some more. My sentences were awkward and lifeless. I took to my faithful personal notebook and wrote out my writer's block and sent a copy to my agent, and to my editor, who came late in May. Almost his first remark was, "Alec doesn't live in your marriage. He's not real. Work on that." I asked him if I could go on using the first person, but said that I was so sick of myself and the pronoun "I." He gave me full approval. The work was getting serious now, and the deadline impending. So much, so much to be done. Christ, there isn't time!

CHAPTER 28

La Giaconda and I (Eye)

PALMING MY eyes one day to rest them, searching for a quiet and loved scene, I saw something totally different. I could not sort out my emotions. I was standing outside myself, looking at my disfigurement. I saw myself as in a mirror, and there within the steadily dimming left eye, I saw within the lens a bright-eyed, curious, and merry little girl in miniature, as through the wrong way of a telescope, looking out eagerly before the lid closed on her. The other eye I saw as one black hole or pipe leading straight to my unconscious, a kind of royal road to be explored.

My reaction was delight. I could look inward with the missing eye and look outward intently, peeringly with the still viable one. This was not quite a revelation — rather, it was the ticket to the future, and gave a sense of hope and direction. Oedipus couldn't see until he blinded himself.

There is nothing mystic about me, I being an everyday person who is, however, learning to listen and see — by not seeing — what has been there all the time. Would I dare? I've been blind so much of my life. Now perhaps I could see more fully with a sightless eye.

Looking in, I wondered again about the wink. Was it saying,

"Look out for the real Harriet Stevens when she awakens?" Or could it be freedom at last from my tie to Mother?

Or was it the bizarreness of the whole formal wedding, Mrs. Robey's wedding, and the pomp of its rituals and rites?

Or with my sexuality forced into the purity of a string of matched pearls, with my body now boiling more and more out of control, yet terrified of sex — I know what's going to happen tonight but I don't know anything — was I in a panic? Or was I suspicious that the passion that had come so suddenly wouldn't last — a prescience of my woman's fate to come — and did I wink out of bravado?

Or was it at the moment George Angier Gordon said so pontifically, ". . . the dreadful day of judgment when the secrets of all hearts shall be disclosed," and there were the barn man and Uncle Tom still repressed in my mind. If the Reverend Gordon only knew!

Heretofore my favorite marriage in literature had been in Dickens's *Dombey and Son*, where Florence Dombey and Walter Gay, after all their maturing hardships, walked so quietly hand in hand through the byways of streets to the mossy old church to be quietly united.

> . . . she, as innocent and earnest-hearted — he, as frank, as hopeful, and more proud of her — Florence and Walter, on their bridal morning, walk through the streets together. . . .
>
> The childish feet of long ago did not tread such enchanted ground as theirs do now. The confidence and love of children may be given many times, and will spring up in many places; but the woman's heart of Florence, with its undivided treasure, can be yielded only once, and, under slight or change, can only droop and die. . . .
>
> But through the light, and through the shade, they go on lovingly together, lost to everything around; thinking of no other riches, and no prouder home, than they have now in one another. . . .

Lovingly and trustfully, through all the narrow yards and alleys and the shady streets, Florence goes, clinging to his arm, to be his wife.

"The woman's heart can be yielded only once, and, under slight or change, can only droop or die." *Why did I wink?*

I gritted my teeth.

In a sort of plea, I looked at my picture of La G. She obsessed me. I needed to talk with her, and my mind went on a search for the truth in her. I palmed my eyes again.

This time I went again to the shore, where I was born in midsummer, so long ago, where tides rise and fall and rise again, where I could feel the rhythms and cycles of my body and sense the southering sun, where I could see sunrises and sunsets, where everything beneath my feet was solid granite covered with thin soil, where once I saw a full setting moon, so pale, so pale, at the same time as, when I turned my head, I saw the full rising red sun on the horizon. And I could remember standing on the hillside outside the house, about four o'clock on one early July morning. There in the dark, I heard no sound whatever. There was no one stirring on the road, on the sea. I was too far away to hear wavelets. It was still night. As I waited, a faint color came in the eastern sky. The stars above were fading. Still no sound. I listened. There it came from the east and with the light, almost inaudible at first, a distant muted murmur. It was the pulse of hundreds of birds, way off, beginning the day. Now it swiftly grew louder, more defined, nearer, as it swept westward with the day, flying on from Rockport across Cape Ann over Dogtown to where I stood.

The whole sky was lighter now, although the ground was yet in deep shadow. And then the sound rose to a distant chorus. There was a sudden chirp nearby, a song, and then another and another, and then a carol. And almost at once, all around, the birds were aroused to their full voice. The day had begun.

And so it was I went in fantasy to that spot on the beach where I had stood eighty years ago and saw myself for the first time. The memory was sharp, living. I was then allowed alone on the sand at low tide. The house was still sleeping — it was early, early morning. The tide was way out, and on the far side of the stretch of sand as it met the granite neck of land with its bare ledges rising up, lay lots of small rocks, seaweedy and barnacled. I tilted some up to look for tiny newborn crabs and multilegged pale worms, my eyes loving the miniature. I had never yet looked into the distance. One stone, too heavy, slipped back — plop — into the ooze, and splashed mud onto my clean dress. My *last* clean dress. I should have put on yesterday's dirty one. I straightened, and a wave of awareness and aloneness engulfed me simultaneously. I saw little Harriet standing there, a bad girl again, and I looked out and up and in. I *was* a little Harriet, and there was only immensity. I didn't focus on the pier across the little bay; I saw only the ocean out there, a gray ocean and a gray sky, all one. I was too little! I had discovered myself and looked down at my dress.

I was there again, an old woman now, and I went at dusk, down to that corner of the beach in the shadow of the granite cliffs. More rocks were exposed than when I was a girl, and they were covered with mussels, and there was less sand. I looked out and with my dim eye I saw a fog bank moving in.

And there, suddenly before me, was La G. Her face was clear against that primordial background of rock and water. I looked at her eyes. She stared me down.

"Ah," I sighed.

"Yes, I came. You've soiled your dress."

"Yes, and a lot else . . . I need help. I'm depressed. I feel like hell, and I'm stuck in my writing. Why? Why? And I can't cry."

"What else is new? Come on!"

I was silent.

"You're angry and guilty."

I stiffened. "I'm not. It's pain and nausea. Oh, yes, I'm angry at surgeons."

"Don't be stupid. You're guilty about your dress."

"I think I've shaken the guilt . . . and I've made peace with Mother — "

"Good. You can see in her the same things you've seen in yourself. Fear and anger and love. She also was the All of woman."

"But tell me, and this is important. Why did she shave me the night before the wedding?"

She shook her head a little sadly. "I'll give it straight. You were a sexy little bitch. Sugar and spice. You frightened her. She couldn't stand the smell of sex. She never could, could she? Not even when you were a baby."

"Yes. You know, I still can feel the joy and fun of squeezing the diapers between my legs, or touching with my fingers."

"So you only had an orgasm when you wanted a child. Your body spoke. Except for then, you couldn't be lusty, earthy, wonderfully flushed and beautiful in the act."

I sighed. She went on.

"Don't get me wrong, and don't blame your mother. Men *do* want women to be their possessions, alone. And even you know that some women can be as rampant as men can be raunchy. But that isn't the way your mother — your matriarchy — likes to do things. I'm sorry to say that clitoridectomies are more their style."

"Ah," I said. (What else could I say?)

Then, next, "Why did I wink at my wedding? I've tried to figure out, but nothing quite clicks."

Her laugh was warm. "You'll get it in time. I think you will." She was silent. Then:

"Now what about Alec?"

"I've buried him," I responded.

"Yeah, you buried him. You buried him with anger and resentment. Is that the way to bury someone you love?"

I looked out. The fog was nearer. And I felt its cold dampness.

"Damn it, you can't even make him real when you write about him. That's why you're blocked."

She confused me. I expected her to be a lady, like Mother, who would never have said, "Damn it."

My mind flashed back to my earliest social-work days, when a case took me to the Italian district to visit a mother who had come to the clinic because her little Tony, aged five, wasn't eating enough. The child was straight out of an Italian painting, beautiful and dark-eyed, his head ringed with short black curls. He was quite plump. And there, in their tenement flat, I met the tiny grandmother in the kitchen, which was redolent with a flavorful spaghetti sauce. She wiped her hands on her apron before greeting me. She spoke almost no English, though she had been thirty years in the States, and her daughter interpreted for her. Her brown and wrinkled face was strong, authoritative, and wary. Her gray hair was pulled tight into a bun, showing a fine forehead. White hairs grew on her chin.

I told her Tony was beautiful and that he would be a fine man with many sons. When had she come to America? Could she remember whether it was scary? And how many children had she had? Her face saddened. Three sons she had lost, one in the war, one in an accident, and one was — was away. Emotions contorted her face.

Acceptance of me grew, and soon we smiled as woman to woman. Suddenly she gave an order to her daughter, who said, "She asks you to stay and eat with us." I knew this to be a rare honor that I must accept. The other grandchildren ran in, stared at me, ran out, and ran in, until the meal was ready. Another place was set at the large kitchen table.

"Vino, *the* vino," she said sharply, and her daughter disappeared into a back room and came back with two dark bottles. The great pot of unbroken spaghetti was put on the table. The grandmother sat at the head. The children slurped the strings in. They giggled, then shouted with laughter, as I tried to do the same. Then they taught me. We grew hilarious. The wine was sharp and heady. I'd never enjoyed such a meal before.

We were almost through. The grandmother got up, took the bottle, and with a gesture of refinement, lifted my glass in her gnarled hand, and with delicate motion poured me more as if she and I were great ladies. She set it down gently.

A man appeared in the doorway. She looked up, gave one tremendous scream, ran to him shouting, "Angelo, mio bambino! Mio bambino," hugged and kissed and slapped and hugged him again, and laughed uproariously. Then she stood back and burst out in a flood of Italian that held rage and reproach and bitterness, while he stood with bowed head. As suddenly, again, "Mio bambino," she hugged him, weeping. His arms encircled her now. It was the son who was "away."

I left without notice in the total pandemonium of the family.

Earthy, I thought. Loving, exuberant, angry, tender, with full life force and spontaneity, all the richness that the refined have lost.

La G read my thought. "We don't show our feelings. And we don't soil our dresses. What's so bad about a dirty dress? You're still guilty about it. You're stuck."

"Yes, I'm stuck. And I'm scared. And if I'm not growing, I'm dying."

"What about Alec?"

"To hell with Alec. What about me? I can't do anything right. I don't fit. I'm different. My children ask each other, 'What's Mother up to now?' "

"Isn't that like your Italian grandmother?"

I looked straight into her eyes. "What?" I said.

She held my stare and I held hers.

186

"That Italian grandmother expressed her feelings her way. Didn't you do the same in your way?"

I remembered my impulse to skip to the barn, the jump into the swimming pool, the *Zuleika Dobson*, the appendectomy — a million times I followed my own whim.

"The wink," I said.

Slowly she lowered her left eyelid, held it for what seemed an eternity, and raised it again. Her smile seemed to broaden almost imperceptibly.

"What the hell is wrong with that?"

"Nothing, but . . . oh, all right. Nothing."

She went on. "Another problem of yours is that you won't let yourself be sorry for yourself. You won't grieve for your lost eye. You're depressed. You spend your time pitying others. But you're really angry at their weaknesses. Why not include yourself in the crowd? And about men in particular. Look at what they suffer. All the time. Little hates, big hates, little hurts, big hurts."

"More than women?" I asked.

"No. Differently from women. Why does that surprise you? A man is in one big dilemma. How to be the warrior, the parfit gentil knight, the lord and master, the food producer, driven by the stress of the marketplace, whether in the assembly line in fear of losing his job, or going up the ladder in a big corporation. . . . Every day he must go out to battle, and every moment he wants to go home. And he's been caught, since his first attachment was to his mother, his first indentification was with her, and he has to go out and be pure male. 'Big boys don't cry.' His natural sensitivity is closed to him, except in his first passionate love. That's why he has been so often unresponsive to the emotions of others — he can't look at his own. He's torn. So, of course, he dies sooner than woman, of stress."

I tried to explain to La G all the things I'd been seeing in myself, and that I'd been searching out all the evil women from

187

Lilith to Lizzie Borden. I told her that the seeds of all of them were in me.

"Naturally. All the evil women in history have hated men. Cat and dog; natural enemies. You've made Alec the dog. . . . You're the cat, secretive. Kipling knew. Wanting to walk by your wild lone."

"But he loved me."

"Did you appreciate him?"

"I tried to."

"Trying isn't enough."

"I was a good wife."

"Not good enough."

"I didn't expect you to be so tough."

"You called me, my dear. When someone calls, I come. You called me when you winked, but you didn't know it."

I realized that I was standing in water, and the tide was rising fast. I moved up to perch on a rock. She was still there before me.

"I grew to love him. I really did learn to love him."

"As a narcissistic bitch, you loved him. You resented him as a man."

"Oh please, not that bad."

"No, not that bad. . . . Now, what about guilt? You've let the red thread of guilt run through your life. From you I'm asking now the red badge of courage."

"And I'm betraying myself and Alec by writing this book."

"You're afraid of sharing your truth, like everyone else."

"Don't you have any sympathy?"

"Plenty. But all I care about is the real self. Can you laugh a good belly laugh? Can you cry without holding back? Can you scold like a fishwife? No, the capacity to express your feelings freely was trained out of you."

Suddenly I felt in my body my head-banging as a child and

my screams of rage, and my shouts of laughter at my jack-in-the-box.

Again she read my thought. "Of course, we can't go loose all over the place. We have to become loving and considerate adults."

"But why can't I get close to people? It's as if they'd possess me or I'd possess them."

"Because you *think* they have to possess you, or you them."

"Oh." I looked away.

"Piss or get off the pot," she said.

The fog was on us now.

And she was gone.

But the fog was lifting as I picked my way home with my cane in the dimness, feeling as if I had been talking with some know-it-all psychiatrist. Did I hear a light laugh in the distance, a soft voice saying, "You've been talking to yourself, remember?"

CHAPTER 29

Alec Remembered

OW I was back in my room in Lincoln, reverie over, back in reality. I felt both free and lonely, as if I wanted to laugh and cry at the same time. It was a moment of aloneness so intense and painful it seemed to lift my body out of my room, my house, my environment, and into the cosmos, as if I were out of time and space, as if I were not. In that moment of panic I found myself saying, "Don't run away, go with it!" and the terror changed to a feeling of exquisite joy, a moment known only once before when Father died. And then I was my everyday self again. I determined to get off the pot. I thought of Alec. I could see him clearly now, and started to write.

I saw him in his child's bedroom, with his two imaginary playmates, Singsa and Poonce. While he would never tell what characters these two were, there was always deep joy in his face when he referred to them. With them he must have led a secret life of great adventure; they probably got into all the mischief that an imaginative and sometimes angry child could invent. Of course, outside his room, he did what he was trained to do.

As a small boy, he stuttered extremely badly and in his embarrassment at not being able to get words out, he was quite ingenious in finding a solution. As soon as he could use a dictionary, he would search for an alternative to the word he stuttered on. He became fascinated with words, and through the years, he wore out two Webster's unabridged onion-skin dictionaries, for he was rough with the delicate pages. His vocabulary was extremely broad and he liked new words like *muliebrity* and *steatopygous* — these he would use with attractive women, usually much to their bewilderment.

Behind his brownstone row house was the typical backyard. A shed in the corner held the ash barrels, firewood, brooms, and shovels. Other than the clotheslines, some old flower pots, and a small tree, it was barren. In the winter, the chore man would shovel the snow into a pile in the corner. One storm produced a record fall. The mound of snow was huge and Alec and a boy from down the block built an igloo inside it. One day, after the other boy went home to lunch, Alec was clearing a little further and the entire structure collapsed on him, pinning his knees to his chest, his elbows to his sides, and his hands in front of his face. He shouted for help until he realized he couldn't be heard. As time passed, he could feel himself getting sleepy and also very thirsty. In desperation, he later told me proudly, he bit the back of his hand and sucked the blood, leaving a large scar for the rest of his life. Then, before it was too late, he clawed the snow in front of his face with his fingers, finally freeing up an arm, and scratched a hole to the outside. It was the cook, looking out the kitchen window for him when he did not come in promptly for lunch, who saw this little, red, slowly flopping object sticking out of the snowpile. She screamed for help and Alec was extricated, alive but weak. For the rest of his life, when it began to snow, he would start clearing it away. Large storms troubled him deeply and he was almost irrationally compulsive about *shoveling.*

During adolescence, he was invited to all the coming-out parties and various girls became enamored of him. If he showed particular interest in one, however, his mother had her to the house, and the devaluation afterward was such that he did not see that girl again.

The summers were spent in Stonington, Connecticut, where his mother always rented the same house. It was the classic summer of the era. There were sailing, swimming, and tennis at the yacht club, along with many parties. Ambidextrous, he played tennis with either hand and wielded a wicked racket with all his strength but sometimes less than total accuracy.

He grew to be a striking man, six feet three inches tall, hair brushed straight back from a low forehead, wide eyes, two deep forceps scars, a rather sensual mouth with a lift to the right side and the left caught in the paralysis of his birth injury. The erectness and thrust of his chest made him what I later learned to call a "macho man." Every movement was powerful, strength emanating from whatever motion he made. That strength lasted practically until his death. I early decided that there was so much unexpressed aggression in him that his muscles were always stimulated in a need for violence which could never be fulfilled. Vigorous! Strong! Doing things mightily! He was the "cave man" par excellence. On the face of it he was a brute. Once Alec squeezed me so hard it forced a cry. "Don't you ever do that again," I said after a gasp. "Don't ever, *ever*, or you'll lose me." He never was rough with me again.

He trained in the ROTC at college and when World War I came, he went to Plattsburg, New York, and was commissioned a second lieutenant. The day he was scheduled to go overseas, the armistice was declared. It was then, he later confessed, he wept bitter tears; his chance to be a warrior, and a great one too, was lost.

In those days a man did not work during the summer until he finished college. Once or twice, Mrs. Robey took him abroad and it was on one of these trips, when he was sixteen, that he started the boulder rolling down the mountain.

The year he graduated from Harvard, and before going on to business school, he had his first summer job at some company where he did up parcels all day. It required the kind of precision and perfection he seemed to have enjoyed and his later teaching of me and the children in the proper method of tying up a parcel was exquisite.

His lifelong work at the family-owned mill was not an ideal situation, although it could have been potentially good. The mill, the U.S. Bunting Company (in its early days, the sole contractor to the government for pure wool bunting for flags), was first owned by my great-grandfather, but later my father and Uncle Tom bought shares and ran it extremely successfully. It consisted of a series of low buildings, each containing one element of the stages of textile manufacture, from the raw clipped wool to the finished bolts of beautiful and very fine worsteds. At one time, under my father's guidance, it had the highest record of long-term employees of any factory in the country. Each individual and his problems was known to my father and each was adequately paid; no union was ever able to gain entrance.

Sometimes on Saturday mornings, Alec would take the boys down with him when he went to the office. They remember happily running around the buildings in the skein dollies, looking at the silent complicated machines, feeling the fine lanolin everywhere, and recalling these as one of their happy childhood episodes.

Alec once took our firstborn, Sandy, up in a hired airplane and flew around the countryside, and on another occasion, out on some large government vessel resting momentarily in Boston Harbor and open to the public. The other children were not as lucky.

Alec could be very impatient with them all. When Sandy was in the early grades, he was having difficulty with his homework. Alec would help him with the first problem but then make

Sandy do the second one aloud. Sandy had an unrecognized dyslexia, a disability that was not even named until decades later, and when he stumbled over even the reading of the problem, Alec would be very severe with him, scolding him, telling him he was dumb, and leaving him crying.

Once, there was some candy in a dish on the living room table. Sandy ate some one day without permission and Alec caught him at it. Putting Sandy in the car, Alec drove down to Page's Candy Store in the center of Lowell and bought a one-pound box of the pink and white and yellow bonbons. Back home, he then sat Sandy down and told him to eat the whole pound nonstop. Sandy tried, eating more and more slowly until he suddenly vomited. That was one lesson not soon forgotten.

There was Alec's workshop. It grew with the years and his skills. In his childhood he had not had an opportunity to use tools; the chore man did everything. In our first house, he began by hanging pictures. As his confidence grew and his supply of tools increased, he bought a small green portable metal toolbox. In our second house, the renovated granite stable, he refurbished what had been the original brick-lined manure pit in the basement with the door opening out to the lower level, built a workbench there, hung up his tools, acquired more, and worked out some little inventions such as a mechanical gadget that closed our bedroom window, turned on the coffee, and set off the alarm all at once.

The third home, the rented house in Cambridge, gave no encouragement for either workshop or repairs with the exception of minor electrical or handtool work. However, the fourth house (and the first that we had personally owned) had a fine basement space where the old coal bin had stood. There Alec created a glorious workshop, with a large new table saw, and cupboards around the walls. His tool cabinet in particular was one I rarely touched unless he asked for a tool from it. Every imaginable space in it had its own little holder, rack, or support for practically everything that could possibly be needed. Each had its place and with his eyes shut, he could find any one of them by feel.

The tools were his joy. One after another he accumulated things he needed and eventually became a minor electrician, a part-time plumber, a repairer of anything small or big that needed fixing, and a creator — not of fine cabinetwork — but of utilitarian things like a dressing table, corner cupboards, whatever. They were done with precision and a kind of art. Often he would go to bed stuck on a problem of "how to" but always in the morning he woke up having come up with the right answer in his sleep. He could hardly wait to get to the shop. Here was his heaven. Here he could lose himself.

We worked together on pieces of driftwood, just at that time coming into vogue as art. I was Mrs. Art, he was Mr. Craft. This was truly a joint enterprise which ended by our selling many objects at the Society of Arts and Crafts in Boston. Wherever we went — Florida, Bermuda, New England — the shores and lakes yielded many pieces of beauty.

His last workshop in Lincoln was magnificent. We took the two-car garage attached to the house and made one quarter of it into a storeroom. The second quarter was given to my department with paints, driftwood, and art supplies. In the other half of the space, he set a large window right above his workbench, which now contained his table saw, a drill press, and planer, as well as all his hand tools.

One year Alec ran a little class on home repair. On our back private road were about eight or ten houses altogether. These contained a half dozen preadolescent boys. On Friday nights, these boys would arrive, bearing twenty-five cents and some article from their house that needed repair. Alec was in his element, showing each child how to think out first how the repair might be made and then giving them the tools or materials plus the support and, if necessary, the directions to complete the job. He could not do that with his own children.

Then there was his acting. It began in a small way when we moved to the Lowell house. Alec had never acted before. It seemed suddenly as if his childhood imaginary play with Singsa and Poonce was translated into the real world. He no longer was Alec Robey but a totally new self; he lived the part as the true actor does. After the first play or so for which I read the cue lines to him, he was able to visualize the scenes and needed no help from me. He learned a part extremely fast. On the stage, he was magnificent, whether it was a bit part or not. He was patient and steady and the rest of the cast adored him. He needed no coaching.

The Lowell Players were first, for at that time all the small communities had their acting groups. In Cambridge, he acted in the Cambridge Dramatic and the Belmont Players groups. In Lincoln, it was with the Concord, Lincoln, and Wayland groups. As long as there was character in a part, no matter how small, he became that character. I remember two plays, probably because they created such emotional stirrings in me. One was *Papa Is All,* in which he played the lead, a violent and sadistic Amish father with a damaged leg. Alec had an extra heel attached to his shoe, creating a lurching limp, and with his portrayal of sadism and hatred, he was terrifying in the role.

The other play, *Death Takes a Holiday,* was superb, and he repeated the role with many different groups. His height, his slim erectness, his thrown-back head, his absolute majesty, made him a god, Death.

Death takes a twenty-four-hour holiday and comes to Earth to find why people fear him. During that time, nothing grows older or dies; even nature stays the same. He appears as a visiting nobleman at a sophisticated European weekend. No one suspects that he is Death. His serious grace and charm, his suavity, enchant everyone, and yet a pervasive anxiety grows and all become a little afraid of him. One watches from the audience as the subtle changes among the players occur.

Within that twenty-four hours, he and a clear-eyed lovely young girl fall in love. When Death leaves at the end of his "holiday," when he has seen and sized up the attitude of the people toward death, his goodbye to the girl is tender. She pleads to go with him; to stop her, he tells her who he really is. She replies that she has known it all along but still must go with him. That height, majesty, strength, and fineness are melded into a quality of tenderness and longing. It is breathtaking as he surrounds her within his great black cape with its crimson lining, and the two depart together. And he says, "My love, my little love." I cried as I watched. Of all his plays, his mother came only to these two, and left abruptly before the end of both.

His third joy was rocks. At the beach, granite lay just under the topsoil. After all the original trees had been cut off for lumber, farming had been very meager, and long before my great-grandfather bought the property, it had been turned to pasturage. The early settlers had quarried the granite for use as sills and steps and the poorly split rock was occasionally used in walls. At first we rented and then bought the old farmhouse from my parents and Alec began building new walls and terraces. He got working with bigger and bigger granite hunks. His eye was perfect because he could pick from an old wall or our rock pile exactly the right stone of the right angle. Usually I labored with him, for such work needed two if a stone was heavier than even Alec could lift.

The heaviest crowbar available, with a large iron pipe about twelve feet long pushed over it for a proper fulcrum, provided incredible leverage, and power oozed from him. He was Atlas. We worked as a smoothly operating team. He would move the slab of granite a bit and I would place the chocks to hold it in its new position. Those days of rock work were wonderful and companionable fun. Our many creations still stand, for they were built to last. Did he ever consciously think of that boulder he had rolled down the Swiss mountain?

As the children grew older, could communicate better, and showed interest in Alec's interests, they became people to him. They remember how he taught them, when emotionally stirred, to squeeze the lacrimal glands with thumb and forefinger, as he did himself, so tears would not appear. He later was very proud of two doctor sons, and even went to their graduations, the first such milestone in his children's growth ever.

However, he gave short shrift to his daughter. When she was about four or five and I was learning about parent-child relationships in my analysis, I asked him to take Harriet on his lap just once. "It would mean so much to her." He did and momentarily held her there stiffly; she must have sensed his discomfort and quickly got down. That was that. A decade later, when she first began dating, he complained about the wishy-washy type of boys she went out with. I asked him again to tell her she was pretty and good. He did, and the type of boy changed. She married a man not unlike her father. After his death I was surprised to discover in his wallet a carefully laminated picture of her in her teens which he had evidently carried for nearly thirty years.

For the first ten years of our marriage stress showed in his physical condition. A little scratch could turn into a roaring infection, in those days treated with only hot flaxseed poultices. He had pneumonia once. He had two mastoidectomies; the bone got infected and had to be chipped away. Result: two big dents behind his ears. I would date his improved health from the time the break was made from his mother after Harriet was born, and she would not communicate with him for three months.

Then he felt relief even though her hurt and grieving and loving letters still came; and during my analysis he was even able to talk back to his mother.

I think it was then his "indigestion," or cardiospasm, began. This was a miserable condition. His esophagus between his tonsils and stomach would go into an extremely painful spasm and he could neither swallow nor release air. Nor could he eat anything whatever. The condition would go on for twenty-four to forty-eight hours before it eased. In a way it was like his conflict in stuttering. As if he were a child, he couldn't get anger and frustration out. He cramped. I learned to ask, "Anything I've said or done that's upset you?"

"No."

"Something at the mill?"

"Not that I remember."

"Anything about the children?"

"Don't think so."

"Well, what about your mother?"

"*Yes!*" And he would speak of a telephone call or a letter. He never seemed to learn to do this himself.

His whole body relaxed and the seizure was over at once. After his mother's death he never had another attack.

Except for these early setbacks, Alec's general health was excellent. He saw his doctor yearly, and came back saying, "I'm fine." He liked his three meals a day, had certain preferences, couldn't stand the slightest color of pink in his meat, had his two drinks at noon and two or three at night, slept within ten seconds of the time his head hit the pillow, and did not wake for at least eight hours. He liked me in contact with him, but was able to tolerate my reading or writing in the middle of the night if I couldn't sleep. He appeared not to wake, but there was a faint sigh from him as my body touched his again.

Like his mother, he never spoke of pain until the day he died, when he said his bones ached. (Mrs. Robey proclaimed that she loved to go to the dentist and have her teeth drilled, the buzzing sound was so pleasant. She never would accept novocaine.) I never ever heard Alec mention pain. Once a large log he was splitting misbehaved when he struck a knot and the heavy iron wedge slipped and slammed down on his big toe. He did not speak of it until the next day when he couldn't get a shoe on, and we found the toe was broken. Was his freedom from pain stoicism or was it natural morphine? Bravado?

About once a year he developed on his left wrist a round, white cancer spot. Each time when it reached a certain size he would take a burning cigarette and press it upon that white spot until the cigarette went out. The spot healed and his treatment was successful year after year. "Doesn't that hurt?" I asked.

"Not a bit," he said. He did have some aspirin in his medicine closet through the years, but no other medicine of any kind.

After we moved to Lincoln, there in the woods where the snow lay deep, he would urinate outdoors, and it was to my infinite fury and envy that he would write in the pure white his initials, A.A.R. It was the periods that were the most annoying.

Republican he was born and Republican he died. I became a Democrat, with occasional reservations, when I went into social work. I was able to persuade him to vote for John F. Kennedy, and he was watching TV when Kennedy was shot. When the final news came, the tears rolled down Alec's cheeks for a long time and he cursed freely and repetitively.

He would never bet. I loved making bets and would try it ten to one or one hundred to one on almost anything. But he always refused my wagers. When, however, his son-in-law from West Point asked him to bet twenty-five cents on the Army-Harvard game, he accepted. The bet became a yearly ritual and, if he won it, that twenty-five cents seemed to be worth a million.

Just as he hated the word *Democrat,* he hated the word *fairy.* And his revulsion was so extreme as to be suspicious.

After his seventies, he still gave the impression of great strength, still crushed people's hands, but had less energy for heavy work. We still had projects, however.

The cruel little curl to the right corner of his upper lip and his stuttering had long since disappeared. He stopped fussing over misplaced keys or lighters. The scars on each side of his face simply became unnoticeable wrinkles. His hair, now snow-white, thinned only a little at the temples. He brushed it straight back so his head was as handsome as of old.

His haircut was absolutely the same for fifty-two years. No way could I get him to let it be just a little longer in the back and not so clipped. He spoke with some indignation of the change in fifty cents a cut to five dollars during his lifespan.

His teeth were always very soft with many fillings and one by one, apparently without any root pain, they fell out. At first it was one bridge, then another, then a lower plate, then an upper one so he had a full set of false teeth. Rarely would he take them out in my sight. But even with the teeth in, his face lost some of the power and charm. Aggression seemed to have faded from his face along with the teeth.

His hands in his seventies were not knobbed by any rheumatism, although one little finger did curl inward. They were hands that should have been drawn by an artist with the dark veins showing through the thinning skin and the muscles practically visible. The power, the great power, was still there in them.

Though he held the same weight, his abdomen grew a little prominent as he grew older, which made his back sway a little bit. His eyebrows were white and bushy. His smile had become tender — most of the time. Glad to have his children appear, he could talk about ideas with them.

One of our freighter trips took us around Africa and up to Madagascar and then Mombasa. On the way back, three days out of New York, with too much to drink, he slipped down some circular stairs. It was rapidly obvious that some ribs were damaged. The second mate strapped him up, we landed in New York, we drove to our daughter's in Greenwich, Connecticut, and there a car met us and took us home to Lincoln. He sat rigidly upright all the way. Although rather quiet, he mentioned nothing about discomfort. The X-rays showed that five ribs were broken through and also that he had emphysema. He was re-bound up and never smoked another cigarette.

So who was he, this man of mine? He came as a warrior comes, all power, poetry, and adoration. And he became a survivor. He made a virtue of what he was, with that body one great torque of power, and his hidden rage stimulating his muscles that so rarely had an outlet for action. All his life his mother, his female Svengali, rode his shoulder. But he was scared. His outstanding external feature was his immense power, but it only covered his constant, fundamental fear.

He had a human craving for order — that order by which laws have brought some permanence and continuity. His own laws were essential to his security, which was a perilous one in marriage. For him time must stop to keep the sameness. Time makes events follow each other. And time brings death. And with an impulsive wife and four healthy children, there could be no order and sameness. So he yelled his hurt only at things or at situations that threatened that precarious serenity of his. His masculinity was always at risk, but he reasserted it with his handshake.

There was a sense of reliability, of dependability, in his own growing creativity; the joy for me was being a partner in such pleasure.

It's interesting that the years of his mother's social indoctrination never took. He was totally unselfconscious. He had not the slightest awareness of what people thought of him, or if he did, he didn't care. Nobody was "anybody" or "somebody." He had a much better time kidding with the boys in the grocery store than he did with people at elegant parties, which he disliked.

I thought again of his sobs on our wedding night. Was it having to be a master to a timid, gentle woman when he had never been allowed to master? One wonders if a sentence in the 1938 letter from Isabelle suggests one effort at working away from her in adolescence, an attempt he obviously lost. After having always been told what to do, he married a woman waiting wide-eyed for his wishes to be expressed so that she might fulfill them. That must have been awful for him.

He put his foot down hard only twice in our marriage. The first time he must have been frantic. It was less than two years after our wedding when he insisted we move from our quite luxurious and "free" house so close to my parents and go away, somewhere, anywhere. We were advised by Puss Leaman that we should go to Lowell, close to the mill.

The other time was after my mother died. We were not to go to the shore anymore in the summer. Both these behests were to be obeyed — and without noticeable repining by me. He could stand the beach in terms of my seeing Mother every day in atonement for my winter neglect. But the various relatives there gave an impression and an appearance of being very sure of themselves, and indeed endowed with much more money than we had. Their superiority he could not tolerate.

Alec was so sure and unsure at the same time. But slowly he came alive as an original, and I could see the poetry in his soul emerging through the fear and the male posturing, that poetry with which primitive man looks upon the thing he creates and sees it as good.

When we moved to Lincoln, the first thing Alec bought was a four-wheel-drive jeep with a plow. It was the squattest, squarest, jumpiest little piece of equipment, and because the two brackets out front to lift the plow looked like horns, he named it "Ferdinand," for Ferdinand the Bull, and so it remained, with Ferdinand I and Ferdinand II. He would go all over our land into the bumps and hollows and up the hills, carrying the wood he had sawed to the woodpile and the brush to the burning pile. He also used the jeep daily wherever he went, and for twenty-three years, whenever it snowed, he would gleefully plow all the way out to the main road, clearing some neighbors' drives as he went. He was famous on our road for the way he gunned the motor and rammed the new mass of snow with a great thud into an already high bank. The jeep and Alec seemed to become one, for here he was master of himself, the snow, and the machinery.

On the other hand, one day when he and I were sitting at the breakfast table drinking our last coffee before going to work, he made a momentous remark that I was never to forget. The dining room had glass to the floor on one side. It was early April and overnight the snow had fallen heavily — wet snow that bowed the hemlock branches low almost to the breaking point. The sun was rising and, as it struck our house and the trees, the branches let go of their load and sprang back into place while the mass of snow fell with a whoosh and a faint thud. A very curious expression came on Alec's face. His eyes were looking at the trees but they weren't focused there — they were way off somewhere. He said, "I could sit here all day falling off those trees." In those ten words, he taught me something so important that it has remained vivid in my mind since. He had a sensitivity and mysticism and a oneness with nature that went back to the time when man and nature were not differentiated. Alec had something I did not have and probably would never have — an inner spirituality and beauty that I envied him. For I, at the same moment, was about to say in effect, "Here am I looking at the trees and isn't it beautiful" —

a purely subjective response. From then on, I looked at Alec with a certain awe.

Some forty years ago I was working in a treatment center for disturbed children under five.

I remember a small boy with his first crayons and paper. When asked what the blob he had created represented, he hesitated, said, "A lion," then cried out in terror and tried to run out of the room. He would not go near the crayon shelf again. A little further along in treatment, however, he was able to try once more. This time, his whole being on guard, he again drew his lion, his body as far away as possible from the paper, hesitated as to whether to run or not, and then swiftly drew a big, rough square around it. Bug-eyed but proud, he shouted, "I put it in a cage. I made a cage for it!"

Alec had his lions that must be constantly caged. Yet, as the years passed, he saw that they were not lions after all. I had asked La G why I couldn't get close to people, as if they would possess me or I them and she said that was only what I *thought*. Alec thought it too, but in our lives together we disproved it. We both possessed each other and freed each other. I was off the pot.

CHAPTER 30

Reprise and Reprieve

N JUNE I saw my eye doctor. Further macular degeneration and now a cataract. No wonder I couldn't read large-print typing, magazines, and books any longer. "When the time comes," Dr. J said, "We'll do a lens implant, but we'll delay that as long as possible since there is always a slight risk. Let's not go totally blind."

"Am I legally blind yet?" I asked, thinking of the benefits.

"Not quite."

Late in the month my editor came several times. He had read and reread the manuscript so far, but we did not deal with that. Mostly we philosophized on evil and good, men and women, marriage and life. He was helping me pull together the threads I was unwinding.

At the end of the month I moved to the beach for another summer. My appetite was back (I had lost twelve pounds), but the inability to read my many notes for unfinished chapters left my mind in the confusion of constant frustration even as the drive to finish the book grew more intense. There was still painful emotional work to do.

I found myself shy of relatives there, but that beloved place with its openness and ionized air, and its battle of sea with granite, and the feeling of the presence of La G allowed my mind to function more clearly.

My psychiatrist son and his word-processing computer and his wife and their sheltie stayed with me for a while, helping me out of my discouraging morass. The computer was a cold, ugly, fascinating, and incomprehensible piece, but the sheltie was small, silken-haired, loving, dependent, and totally deaf. In this house the living room leads to the den-bedroom, to the dining room, into the tiny hall — a fine open circle, and each evening, before dusk, if we were inside, that gentle animal went intently and steadily round and round the rooms. He was herding sheep. With dusk he lay down and rested. If we were outside, he chased birds and airplanes, dashing around below them as if he were rounding up the strays.

How many generations of Man since Scotch shelties were trained to herd? How many more generations of dog as pet had been bred, never having smelt or seen a sheep? How long did it take, once upon a time, to train shelties to herd? How long before the training became instinct that drove him to go round and round an old wooden house? And what about us in our own past training and ingraining? Yes, I thought, we have our far more complicated instincts, too, and we too drive and are driven. But we do not have to. We are conscious animals, and I consciously relaxed.

My children, the sheltie, and that terribly hungry computer–word processor departed at the end of July. At the same time, the first draft of this book went to the Atlantic editor. I felt the last part was hurried and incomplete and that I was still trying too hard to get answers from La G, but I must wait for criticism. That might be slow coming, as my editor was on vacation and he is a contemplative man. But the pain of memory in writing was over.

Now there was nothing to do. Nothing? My body itched to get going, and then took over in a sudden rush of energy as my mind went fallow. I started by cleaning all the windows I could reach — they were salt-dimmed from a recent northeast storm and people must look both out and in. Sensing the ground with my staff (the handle of a broken hoe, now rubber-tipped), I went up to the level of the tennis courts and took long strides alternating with mild jogging until I'd reached the heavy panting stage. I did my back and leg exercises more and more deeply until muscles hurt. How could they revitalize so quickly? There was a sense of tremendous energy as if I were no longer locked in the dark of my mind but was in touch with my corporeal self. I went through every cupboard, closet, drawer, so I would know where everything was and that there was nothing unused or unusable. And all the time I was pleased as punch with myself. I even, for the first time ever, used tools in a minor way and found I could do it, instead of waiting for my sons. "Would you do this for me? Would you do that?" Clumsy I was, but at times I was almost drunk with a strange happiness.

Best of all, people again. I loved seeing them approach the house, the porch; I loved the give and take that followed, I loved being just anybody now. Sometimes two great-grandchildren played on the floor near my feet. Love and tolerance and acceptance were so strong in me it seemed as if their ramparts could not be breached.

August heat wave. For three days the oppressive humidity had wilted everyone and each night sheet lightning danced eerily among the clouds. Late on the fourth afternoon heavy thunderheads gathered over the Essex and Ipswich shores. I watched white sails, the white wakes of motor boats scudding for the river. Far across the bay lightning streaks split the black clouds. I counted the seconds between flash and thunder rumble. Now I closed western windows, pulled back furniture on porches, and then settled in my Gloucester hammock on the upstairs porch to watch. Now a sweet little cooling breeze quickly freshening. Now the squall line that even my eyes could see, far across the bay. Now the rain line, blotting out everything behind it. Lightning more brilliant, thunder louder. First raindrops. Then deluge driving before the wind, soaking the whole porch floor to my feet. Now flashes all around almost simultaneous with the deafening crashes of noise. A second of held breath with each one. The fire siren sounded the local number. Some house nearby had been struck.

Suddenly! In answer to a final great flash-crack and its thundering vibrations that shook the old house, I shouted out my own shock waves of four-letter obscenities, earthy words, words of anger and bravado, and . . . an acceptance of nature and the nature of mankind — his pain, his strife, his so rarely found peace and serenity as we sell our birthright for a mess of pottage.

The storm was passing across the cape to the open Atlantic. The last rumblings more periodic, softer. In my body I felt the ending of Beethoven's Pastoral Symphony, quieter . . . quieter. To the west the sun shone suddenly on a suddenly blue sea. Little clouds were pure cotton, the air sparkling, clear, cool, salt-filled. Then there was silence.

The evening was so still, so very still. A last gull mewed and squawked its raucous cry. The thrushes in the windbreak of locust trees to the north side were settling down with their sleepy peeps. The arrhythmic clang of the cumbersome red bell buoy — a half-mile off the point — became musical by distance, that sound so welcome to sailors.

Beyond the low curved stone wall of granite that Alec and I had such fun building, the unmowed grass was a golden carpet. I watched as the sun seemed to hesitate above Hog Island off the Essex shore — was gone. Now the fluffy white clouds above showed their first tinge of pink — the color grew a deeper and deeper rose — the whole horizon glowed . . . faded. The color in the clouds went out. The cicadas ceased their cry. But the light on top of the bell buoy now flashed that faithful rhythmic signal that could not be subdued even by great storms. It was my nightly friend. And wouldn't it be nice if I could be similarly refueled every three years, too? I asked myself at last why the sudden quickening of life.

I thought of La G, also my friend, and asked why she smiled, and asked once more why I had winked and kept on winking through life, and why it was always fun (though maybe not at the time). And these two questions fused. She was what she was, calm and unthreatened. Smiling. Good.

"Good," I said.

My mind went swiftly back to my first professional year of social work in an agency for children under five. I had a client, May Vandergrift, whose little boy of four was brought in with a behavior problem. As she sat in my office, she deliberately flicked cigarette ashes onto the rug, although an ashtray was at her elbow. She was poorly dressed, depressed, and angry, and there was an odd and unpleasant smell about her clothes. I soon found that her husband was a garbage collector — the old-fashioned kind — emptying dripping, stinking pails into a truck. Joe refused to come to the agency, though we needed his help with the child's problem. With permission, I visited their top-floor tenement to meet him there. It was a run-down, ill-insulated flat, terribly hot in summer under the black-tar roof, cold in winter, and heated by two kerosene stoves, on one of which they cooked. A front sitting room, a bedroom and bath, a kitchen with a little room off it where the boy slept, comprised the whole. The place was redolent of kerosene and swill. Joe knew I was coming and sat in the front room with three of his truck pals, all drinking beer. I joined them, was offered a bottle, accepted with thanks, and they kidded me mercilessly about being one of those "do-gooders." Joe said he knew social workers well from childhood. I responded with humor. We all had fun. And when I called him the next week, he agreed to come to my office. But only after five. This was awkward, for the clinic closed then and my office was on the third floor back in the huge old house which the agency occupied. And Joe was reported to be quick with a knife. But after the first visit he came weekly and I ceased being anxious those dark winter evenings.

He told me his life story — slums of New York City, gang fights, kid dreams of being a doctor, and of how he had gathered a simple little medical kit and how, one lucky day, he was present when a man fell splash several stories to the pavement. He rushed up and started to apply first aid. The police at once arrested him. Soon he was sent to reform school, then home, then another school; somewhere he learned something of electricity. He was proud that his ancestors had been the best harness makers in the early days of New York, for the Vandergrifts had come from Holland with that skill and passed it down, generation to generation, until the automobile arrived. Then came poverty, and loss of employment and of pride.

On a navy ship during the war that was struck by a submarine shell but not sunk, he was sent down to the blackened bowels of the cruiser to do repairs. Always terrified of closed spaces, expecting another explosion, he there went berserk. After hospitalization, he was discharged from the navy with 100 percent disability. The outdoor garbage job was the only one he could tolerate or could get.

As we worked together, whenever he had an idea or constructive thought, I called him "Dr. Vandergrift." He loved it. Under my full respect he blossomed.

Meanwhile May, who proved to be capable of considerable insight, dressed more neatly as her anger and bitterness eased, used the ashtray meticulously, and the parents worked together on a less punitive attitude toward their only child.

Several years after treatment May called me. They had moved to a small town well away from the city. She had a job as assistant postmistress, he as an electrician. They had bought one of the little new houses springing up at that time — all alike, all in a row, with a tree on the bit of lawn out front, a picture window with white ruffled curtains draped back, and a lamp on the table in the middle. The kid was doing well in school. She thanked me warmly.

The impact on me of this case — and of others — was tremendous. It was the knowledge that most human beings, given acceptance and respect, "go good." The human soul needed only that help to reach up and out.

Looking out into the night of the sea, I felt that I was now shriven. But not in the usual way. I thought of the conceptualized Christian Heaven, that place of bliss and radiance eternal, but one which, in its sameness, stirs no adrenaline. There would be no sea there, no great breakers that crest to a triumph as they die; no little wavelets that murmur in different sibilants on a rising or fallling tide. Man may alter the face of the land, I thought, but never the oceans that circumnavigate our planet, just as the salt has circumnavigated through our bodies since life began.

Yes, I'd rather end as a bit of wrack upon the shore than a wraith in Paradise; rather feed the fishes than the guilt of my offspring, or watch, from Heaven, as they sweat out the pain of their very humanness; rather end in that still deep darkness where life began. For only the titan oceans have told the lapse of time since time began with the emergence of life.

I was a mother, a grandmother, a great-grandmother, a patient, and a therapist. I didn't feel I'd left undone the things I should have done, and I did always the best I could at the time.

I did not always conform — I winked — but I never deliberately hurt anybody.

I was a neighbor, a friend, an enemy. I had done what I must and in following my healthy instincts I had become unique and so discovered my genius and my originality.

I would never forget La G. She smiled at me. And once she winked at me and I winked back, for I "heard her." And now at last I know why she smiles. Someone, somewhere, has "gone good." Trite? Probably, but it still happened.

What have I found after these two years of often painful work? Nothing that I can say. I haven't found The Truth, or God. And I'm not sure now that I was looking for them, or true beauty, or the Mona Lisa's pure dispassion, or anything.

But I think I've found everything, for I've found myself. At least right now, and I have left behind forever the selves I thought I was. And I felt, as I saw the land and sky lightening with the full moon rising behind the house, that I didn't need to find anything else. Hadn't my song of life been a lilting one? For the first time I could feel as I felt at the altar, quickened. Wasn't that enough?

Impulsively, I pulled out the neck of my blouse and dropping my head down I held the cloth up over my face. And the clean, warm body odor that I breathed in was incredibly, indescribably, hauntingly beautiful, with the whole of everything contained in it. Deeply I inhaled. As it was in the beginning. Ah! Someone should create that particular perfume. It was my mother's smell, and now it was mine.

After a long mental stillness, I floated into my nightgown and into my bed, and with that sudden relaxation of a body serene, I heard myself whisper, "Now I lay me down to sleep."

And now it is the very end of August. The days have had their warning of change and finality. But tonight is mild and still. The threat of a storm to come is evidenced only by a low bank of clouds in the northwest and west. We, a little group of three Robey generations, sit on the grass of the picnic ground, that spot that Alec and I, over forty-five years ago, carved out from a hollow in the uneven ledge that runs from the tennis courts to the pier below. Our granite fireplace has endured and our birthday lobster picnic is finished. We are replete. The jeepload of last winter's wrack, hauled up from the beach by a grandson, constantly refuels the fire and the floating sparks are little stars.

Darkness comes on as we wait for our music-minded relatives from the far corner of the estate, Danny and his guitar being the catalyst for song. Meanwhile we study the night and the sea, all facing west-northwest. Above in the moonless sky the stars are so large and brilliant one wants, like a child, to reach up and touch. We identify some of them. Across Ipswich Bay the necklace of lights defines the horizon. Now and then above us flashing across the sky is a shooting star, traveling into nowhere — gone. The Isles of Shoals light blinks its steady rhythm as it did when I first saw it as a child, so many years ago, a solitary star suspended in nothing. The tide is almost at flood, and the lamps on the big granite dock across the cove send slightly wavering reflections to the rocks below us. Suddenly the rare northern lights are there, rising over the low bank of clouds, flickering upward. Their flowing is as elusive to the eyes and the mind as their color. So, too, it was in my childhood . . .

One by one, silently, from over the smooth lichened ledge behind us, appear young relatives. They drop cross-legged into a circle. The firelight silhouettes heads or brightens faces. Great sparks, like stars, are gone before they land. We wait. Danny touches his guitar, plays a few notes, and suddenly, voices in harmony pick up the song, softly, lightly, tenderly, and the words are *clear*. Here is no shouting out, as in my youth, "I've Been Working on the Railroad," "Clementine," "Oh, Dem Golden Slippers." These songs speak of love and loss and life and death and trivial poignant incidents, the cries of youth becoming adults, and Danny's voice leads the rest. It all seems so clean and clear, and in my dark corner I cry quietly and do not know why I cry. If only Alec were here.

How he loved me! And how I loved — love — him.

The anger I felt after the honeymoon was over stayed with me all the years of our marriage. Alec was an unfeeling brute, who needed *Bartlett's Familiar Quotations* to possess me. He didn't love me, he only cared about possession. But how wrong that was! In that moment when the first sexual passion had become commonplace, real love began, but I missed it, because I was so hurt.

I loved him and he loved me and both were frustrated often by the other's personality quirks, but we permitted each other the space between our togetherness. This is what love is and this is what I weep for as I never thought to weep before. And we gave life to four loving, capable children, steeled by their father and sensitized and made tender by me, as I think it should be, and our genes are in the many grandchildren and great-grandchildren.

Our marriage wasn't the many marriages I tried to list earlier. It was merely two marriages, one as I had read it with narcissistic blinders on, the other as I saw it now, the real marriage that we created. It had been a good one and we had both grown. In marriage we had found each other and ourselves.

Peace and grace.